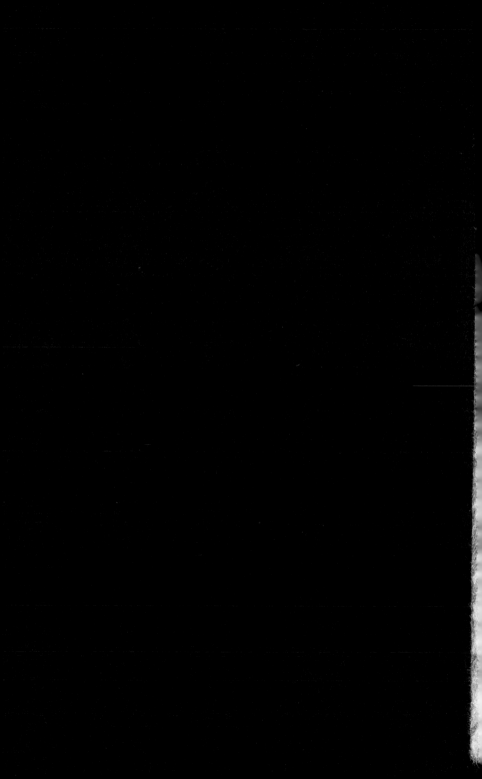

AMERICAN INJUSTICE

AMERICAN INJUSTICE

MY BATTLE to EXPOSE the TRUTH

John Paul Mac Isaac

Liberatio
Protocol

A LIBERATIO PROTOCOL BOOK
An Imprint of Post Hill Press
ISBN: 978-1-63758-684-6
ISBN (eBook): 978-1-63758-685-3

American Injustice:
My Battle to Expose the Truth
© 2022 by John Paul Mac Isaac
All Rights Reserved

Post Hill Press
New York • Nashville
posthillpress.com

Published in the United States of America
1 2 3 4 5 6 7 8 9 10

To my mother and my aunt Kathy
For raising me and keeping me safe.

CONTENTS

INTRODUCTION

One seemingly minor and random computer repair job upended my world, turning it into a nightmare. I never expected that I would become a central figure in a national security threat involving a wealthy and powerful political family, or that the government I once believed in, the government my loved ones had served and fought for, would turn its back on me.

Beginning in April 2019, when Hunter Biden brought three damaged Mac computers into my repair shop, I sought only to do the right thing at every step. And at almost every step, I was met with skepticism, suspicion, and even death threats. I feared for my life, not just in the face of angry strangers but in the face of a hostile FBI.

Intelligence agency directors turned on me. Friends and community members turned on me. Even my customers turned on me. My business might never recover.

And I will never feel completely safe while the world at large continues to see me as an enemy. So this is an attempt to set the record straight, to show that my actions regarding the incriminating laptop were all done in the interest of protecting our great country. That I tried to follow the proper protocols although there was no guidebook. That

I'm not a spy, a Russian hacker, a liar, or an evil person coldly motivated by politics.

"If you see something, say something," we're told. I did see something, and I did say something. I was vilified for it. Hopefully, this true recounting of events will restore my good name and my feeling of personal safety.

Read it and judge for yourself.

THE CALL

October 13, 2020

It's ten minutes until closing, ending another slow Tuesday at The Mac Shop, my computer repair shop in Wilmington, Delaware. I refuse to close early, in case a customer comes in. Tuesday used to be my busiest day of the week; I'd be buried in work. Now, with business about a quarter of what it was before the COVID-19 pandemic hit, I find myself buried in YouTube videos about World War II aircraft instead.

I can't really complain, though. Business has been picking back up since the lockdown was lifted, and unlike many people I know, I never lost my job or had to close. Many of my clients consider me an essential service worker, and I've stayed open for them—even though most of them have been staying away for months now.

I love my shop. It's a twenty-by-forty-foot ground-floor retail unit on the back side of a little multilevel shopping center built in the 1980s. The group of shops is in Trolley Square, about two miles west from the center of Wilmington and home to bars and restaurants as well as stores.

I've put a lot of work into my place, replacing the vomit-colored linoleum with weathered wood-look planks, adding a collection of vintage Apple products affectionally named "The Mac Museum," bringing in an eight-foot palm tree for a splash of color. Framed posters of old Apple products and ad campaigns now adorn the pale gray walls.

The back holds a service-and-storage area. The waiting area at the front has an Apple Genius–inspired bar in light pine laminate with five seats, plus a large gray leather couch. The bar is void of equipment now except for my collection of smaller Apple gadgets displayed at the end. In the past, some days I would be lucky to have a few feet of open countertop to serve new customers. I miss the days when iMacs were lined up front to back on the counter like Rockettes.

When things were busy, I often sat behind the counter behind the seventeen-inch screen of a MacBook Pro. I'd have to locate the store phone by sound instead of sight, and getting my hands on a the right screwdriver could be a challenge.

Behind me on the wall that divides the customer-facing part of the store from the service-and-storage area hangs a fifty-five-inch flat-screen TV. Originally used for training and demonstrations, it's now more a conveyor of Netflix and YouTube videos. Tonight, my back is facing the TV as I watch videos on a smaller screen, optimistically keeping an eye on the door.

The phone suddenly jangles, pulling my attention away from the video. I lean back from my screen and sigh deeply, thinking, "What kind of service is someone expecting to get so close to closing?"

"Mac Shop!" I say cheerily into the phone.

"Hello, my name is George Mesires. I'm a lawyer for Hunter Biden," the voice says.

The world freezes. It feels like an eternity before my heart starts beating again.

"How can I help you?" I finally respond, calmly and clearly.

"My client dropped off some equipment, maybe a laptop, in 2017, and we're checking to see if you're still in possession of it," the man says.

My thoughts flick back to December 2019, when Special Agent Mike DeMeo of the FBI gave me instructions for what to do if someone ever came looking for Hunter's laptop—which was now in the FBI's possession.

"Stall them. Tell them it's in another building and you will retrieve it the following day," Agent DeMeo told me. "Text me and I'll return it to you in twenty-four hours."

Now I tell George, "Normally, we don't hold on to equipment that has been abandoned for that long. I have an offsite location for all of our recycled and abandoned equipment. I can check tomorrow and let you know."

Then, cool as a cucumber on the surface, I try to get something in writing too.

"Just so I know who I am talking to and that you're allowed to represent my client, can you email me your contact information?" I ask. I provide my email and tell him I'll contact him tomorrow.

I'm feeling like I'm handling this well—maybe the adrenaline is fueling my confidence—when he says, "So are you still located on the back side of Trolley Square?" My heart sinks. Before, when George said Hunter had left the computer at my shop in 2017, I thought, "This guy is two years off and can't remember a thing. It was 2019. I might still get out of this somehow." But when he mentions my location, my hope quickly fades and is replaced with fear. I look toward the big windows at the front of the store and realize how exposed I am.

I give George the store address and again tell him I'll look into the abandoned equipment. He thanks me for my time and hangs up. I run around the counter, pull down the blinds, and lock the door. Then I pick up the phone again and call Robert Costello, a lawyer for Rudy Giuliani I've been working with.

"Hey, boss, I just received a call from a man claiming to be a lawyer for Hunter. He asked if I still had the laptop. What do I do?"

"Not much to do," Bob replies. "That ship has sailed." I repeat the conversation with George back to Bob and ask, "How did they find me?"

"It's standard procedure before an article goes to press that those involved would be contacted for a comment," he says. The *New York Post* would be running a story on the contents of Hunter's laptop the next day.

"So, I'm screwed, and they know where I am," I respond.

"Don't worry. Go home and relax," Bob says. "The article is going out tomorrow, and they can't stop it. Call me if you get into trouble. Everything will be OK."

My Mac dings with an email notification. A message from George reads:

John Paul: Thank you for speaking with me tonight. As I indicated, I am a lawyer for Hunter Biden and I appreciate you reviewing your records on this matter. Thank you.

Well, shit. The cat's out of the bag now. I have to get out of the shop, but I can't go home. What if someone is watching the shop? What if they follow me home? All the awful scenarios I've been imagining over the past year return in vivid force. I realize that the same FBI that has been so active in hiding the truth from the American people and protecting the Biden family could easily have handed out my personal information—or worse, could be waiting for me at my house.

I text a friend and ask if I can stay the night, then call for an Uber. I've never been to this person's house, and it's off the radar. I tell myself all I have to do is make it through the night and brace for what the next day will bring. I figure at least with the story's making the news, it will be harder for someone to make me "disappear." I'm trying to be optimistic, but fear and anxiety are creeping in.

I turn off the shop lights and wait in the dark for the Uber to arrive. For most of the ride, I keep looking over my shoulder, wondering if the headlights behind us are following me. For the first time in my life, I have a panic attack.

My heart feels like it's beating out of my chest.

I feel disconnected from my body.

My mind is racing with thoughts of every potential outcome to this: murder, prison, threats and harm to my family and friends—whom I've tried so hard to protect.

Each thought adds another layer of anxiety, pinning me down and pressing against my chest. No air seems to be reaching my lungs.

Finally, I arrive at my destination. My friend gives me a pillow and a blanket for the couch. I try to go to sleep, but sleep is the last thing on my mind tonight. And it will be the same for many nights to come.

PART ONE

THE HANDOFF

A LITTLE BACKSTORY

I was born on May 3, 1976—a pale, hairy, blonde, blue-eyed baby boy. The nurses quickly dubbed me "The White Ape." It wasn't until about five years later that doctors would officially label me an oculocutaneous albino, meaning I have almost no melanin pigment in my skin, hair, and eyes. People with oculocutaneous albinism don't just have very light skin and eyes; the lack of melanin in the eyes results in vision abnormalities. I guess after too many collisions with sliding glass and screen doors, my parents had decided it was time to figure out what was wrong.

Along with the diagnosis came a long list of dos and don'ts, followed closely by expectations and limitations. Needless to say, growing up under these rules was very frustrating. But from this frustration sprouted determination and a will to find a way to do the things people told me I couldn't. Visual communication became a passion. I learned early that I could see a screen more clearly when I sat four inches in front of it. And I discovered I could achieve a level of detail in my artistic creations digitally. Although I had a fondness for ceramics, likely due to the tactile quality, my world opened up when I sat in front of a Mac.

In the summer of 1988, when I was twelve years old, my parents sent me off to live with my aunt Kathy and uncle Neil in Colorado—most likely to give my mother a much-needed break. My aunt was a math teacher in the Denver public school system. She was strict and quick to discipline, but also loves me dearly and has always been one of my greatest supporters. And that summer, she brought home an Apple Macintosh II.

It was the first color Macintosh. It was life-changing.

I could make art on a computer! No more paint on clothes or the carpet. No more forgetting to clean the brushes. And with Apple's assistive technologies, mainly the zoom feature, I could achieve a level of detail I never could have imagined before. Although I couldn't see the details on any printouts, I knew they were there because I could see them on the screen by zooming in.

The Macintosh II was the doorway to a new world, one where I could move around freely. I had just needed the right tools, and the Mac gave me those tools.

Thus began my love affair with Macs. The Mac part of my name is just a coincidence, as with my father earning the nickname "Mac" while in the military. My last name is Mac Isaac, a good Scottish name with nothing to do with computers.

Fast-forward a few decades. At age twenty-eight, I was working as a "lead genius" at an Apple store in Delaware. As part of the leadership team, I was responsible for delivering exceptional customer experiences and helping ensure that all the team members had the tools and support they needed to do so as well, among other things.

After about three years there, when I was thirty-one, I was transferred to a new Apple Store in Littleton, Colorado, about eleven miles from Denver. Until I was able to find a place to live, my aunt Kathy once again welcomed me into her home. I was back living in her basement, but now my uncle Neil had created an utter masterpiece of a living area. And this time I wasn't discovering Macintosh. I was fixing Macintoshes. It felt like coming full circle. I felt a completeness.

Then the Great Recession of the late 2000s hit, causing the focus of your typical Apple Store to shift from service to sales, from fixing and preserving to replacing. But I still wanted to protect customers' investments and not just separate their money from their wallet. I thought there was an opportunity to recreate an Apple Store, but as it was in the golden age of Apple service: no appointments; no time limits; no taking away your beloved or needed Mac for two weeks. And with customer service that started and ended with a handshake, not a web form or a phone call.

Ride-sharing apps hadn't been invented yet, and Denver's mass transit didn't work for me. So I returned to Delaware and opened my own Mac repair shop.

About nine years later, my life changed as radically as when I'd first fallen in love with the Mac. Only this time, it wasn't for the better.

April 12, 2019

It was a Friday night, ten minutes before the shop's closing time. I was checking out a website about computer numerical control (CNC) machines and woodworking. I had no intention of working late; I was ready to go out after a long and busy week. But then bright, cool LED headlights bounced off the counter from the front window. I leaned back in my chair and closed my eyes. My vision of leaving the shop and joining my friends quickly faded as the door chime sounded. As was usual for this time of day, I thought: "What kind of person expects quality service right before closing time?"

I struggled not to roll my eyes when in stumbled a man clutching three MacBook Pros. He was about my height, six feet tall, but a little heavier. He wore casual clothing—dark blue and gray. Alcohol fumes preceded him. He slid the three laptops onto the bar counter as he fumbled for a seat.

"I'm glad you're still open," he said. "I just came from the cigar bar, and they told me about your shop, but I had to hurry because you close at seven."

He looked older than me but had a surprisingly high-pitched voice. An air of entitlement radiated off him.

"Great," I thought. "Another one who thinks the world revolves around them."

To him I said cordially, "You made it just in time."

"I need the data recovered off these, but they all have liquid damage and won't turn on," he said.

"Well, let's get you checked in and see what's going on." One of the computers had a Beau Biden Foundation sticker covering the Apple logo, but I wasn't sure at first whom I was talking to. I opened my customer relationship management software (CRM) and asked him for his first name.

"Hunter," he said.

I then asked him for his last name. He paused and looked at me funny, as if I were from another country and how dare I not know who he was?

"Ah, Biden," he responded, with a sarcastic edge.

I collected his phone number and email, and fed them into the system. Once the paperwork was started, I paused and remembered that this guy had lost his brother, Beau, about two or three years earlier, and I felt a little bad for him. Maybe the Mac with the sticker belonged to his now-deceased brother, and it would bring closure to have access to those memories trapped inside.

On any other night, especially a Friday—being that I was very single—I would have collected the machines and looked at them the next day. For some reason, maybe misplaced compassion, I decided to check them over then and there. One at a time, I performed a quick inspection of the machines. The fifteen-inch laptop was a complete write-off. It had extensive liquid damage, and because the drive was soldered to the logic board, data recovery was beyond my capability. (If a Mac can't power on, you won't be able to access the drive and get to the data.)

The thirteen-inch 2015 MacBook Pro was in slightly better shape. It could boot up, but the keyboard was unresponsive. I pulled out an external keyboard and asked for permission to log in.

Hunter started laughing.

"My password is fucked up. Don't be offended!" he said, before announcing that it was "analfuck69" or something to that extent. His inebriated condition made it difficult to understand is speech. My eyes widened a bit, and I told him that maybe it would be best if he tried to log in himself.

"Hey, you fixed it!" he stated, slurring slightly. I asked if he had an external keyboard that he could use to get around the failure of his internal keyboard, and he just looked at me blankly.

"Here, you can borrow this one to perform the recovery yourself," I told him. "That way I don't have to check it in and bill you. Just bring it back when you're done."

It would have been less work for me that way, and again, I felt bad for this guy. I'd often walked under Hunter's dead brother's name, which adorned the Amtrak station in Wilmington. Beau had been Delaware's district attorney and had died of brain cancer. Aside from that, about all I knew was that he had been the good kid and Hunter was the black sheep. From my own experience as the black sheep of the family, I felt sympathy and wanted to help this guy out.

I moved on to the last Mac, a thirteen-inch 2016 MacBook Pro. The drive was soldered onto the logic board. This one powered on but then would shut down. I suspected that there was a short in the keyboard or trackpad, and if I took it apart, I could at least get it to boot and possibly recover the data.

I explained the repair to Hunter. He agreed to the terms and conditions and signed the paperwork, checking in the computer. I stayed behind as he left the shop. Although it was now well past 7 p.m., I proceeded to take the Mac apart and disconnect the trackpad and keyboard to test my theory. After working on it for about thirty minutes, I was relieved that the machine was able to power on and was mostly stable. I proceeded to inspect the drive. It was 256 GB in size and about 85 percent full. The drive passed its diagnostics, so I decided to perform a clone of the drive to the store server. A clone is a term loosely used to describe a block or sector copy of the drive. If you want to copy a drive in its entirety, you copy the blocks, or physical sectors, of a drive. This copies the data residing on those sectors, both visible and deleted. The process is also incredibly easy and requires only a few clicks of the mouse to set up. I would start the cloning process to run overnight and mop up whatever hadn't made it in the morning.

When I turned off the lights and locked up for the night, I was surprised to see Hunter's big black Ford Raptor truck still sitting in front of my shop, with all of its fancy angles and lighting. I couldn't tell if Hunter was still inside sleeping or what. My focus was on salvaging what was left of my night before coming back in at 10 a.m. the next day, Saturday.

April 13, 2019

Saturdays were my anchor. Out of the six days a week my shop was open, Saturday was the only day that my lunch break was dictated by my own needs, not my customers', and it was different in other ways too. I woke up earlier; I felt an eagerness for the day as opposed to warming up to it slowly in front of YouTube or my phone on the couch. And I walked to work briskly on uncrowded streets, instead of having to navigate the obstacle course of vendors, customers, and everyone else.

I also enjoyed the silence as I walked around the back sides of the shops while being greeted by the blinding sun. It was calming. By the time I turned the key in the lock just before 10 a.m., I felt more prepared to tackle the day than normal. I felt good, ready to start the countdown to the perfect breakfast sandwich.

But on this Saturday, reality kicked in quickly as I remembered the work I had put off from the previous day. I sat down in front of my Mac and opened up the CRM. A quick scroll revealed that out of the five repairs that had come in the previous day, three were awaiting parts and two were awaiting service. Nobody delivers parts on Saturday, so I focused on the other two—one being Hunter Biden's request for data recovery from liquid damage.

Before I could run in the back to check the status, however, the door chime sounded. A senior woman slowly approached the bar, clutching a thick collection of paperwork along with her MacBook Air. I knew instantly that the problem would be passwords difficulty—a monthly occurrence for this customer. Besides data recovery and failing hard drives, resetting peoples' passwords is the most common service I perform.

Luckily, I had memorized her MacBook log-in password and only had to steer her in the right direction today. But again, before I could finish that job and return to

Hunter's laptop, the door chime sounded with a new customer. In walked a man with a twenty-inch iMac with a video card issue. When I explained the problem and the cost to fix it, he decided to just buy a new machine instead of have this one fixed.

I didn't charge either customer, even though I'd spent an hour with them. I have a rule: If I don't have to take a screwdriver to it or have to check it in, I don't bill. To me, it's more important to give free advice and build a relationship than to squeeze a dime out of everyone who walks through the door. Maybe that's why I'm not rich, but maybe it's also why my business had five-star ratings on social media.

Finally, I went in the back to check on Hunter's liquid-damaged MacBook Pro. It had powered off, dying overnight during the file transfer. I now realized that this was not going to be a simple drag-and-drop procedure. There was about three hundred gigabytes' worth of data, but not enough charge in the battery to do it all in one go. I started to charge the unit again, planning to give it a couple of hours before making a second attempt. But I also decided to see what had been successfully transferred to the server, praying I didn't have to start all over again.

The recovered folder was a little over a hundred gigabytes—a third of the total amount needed to be recovered. Seemed like a good start. But when I opened the recovery folder, I saw that only the desktop folder has been transferred.

"Holy shit," I thought. "This guy has a ton of crap on his desktop." There were hundreds of files and photos, and they weren't organized at all, just piled one on top of the other. What a mess!

I changed the folder view to a columns view, to see the files and folders in an alphabetical list. Clicking on a folder in the list opens up a new column with the contents of the folder, and clicking on a file in that column brings up a preview of the file. Eventually, in two separate windows, I would be able bring up both the original desktop and what I had copied, compare them, and transfer the missing files to the recovery window. But first I had to wait until there was enough of a charge in the battery to power on the Mac and keep it on.

And it was getting close to 11:45 a.m., meaning I had a sandwich to order from Angelo's Luncheonette. One of my favorite things about going to Angelo's is the walk. It is a straight shot up the hill on Gilpin Avenue from my shop. You leave the Trolley Square parking lot, cross DuPont Street, and immediately find yourself facing a row of trees straddling the top of a steep hill and a sea of weeds working their way down onto a brick sidewalk. Then you go under a single-track train bridge. This whole area got its name from the long-deceased trolley line that once headed east into the city.

After you pass under the bridge, Gilpin Avenue goes from commercial to residential. It's void of bars and restaurants here except for Angelo's, sitting at the top of the hill. It's a quiet and peaceful walk up to the place, with a smooth and consistent grade—which, being visually impaired, I greatly appreciated. I was used to not asking for help unless I absolutely needed it.

In fact, I became a Mac repair guy despite being told it was too visually intensive for me. I had been working in a café and doing a state vocational program, and heard customers talking about how the Delaware Center for Education and Technology was looking for a Macintosh tech to work in public schools. So I quit my job at the café and moved up to New Castle County with a new job fixing Macs and training educators. After my time with the state, I was sure that if I wanted something done, I'd find a way to do it myself. From there, I went from working at the Apple Bar to being a "lead genius" to opening my shop, proving that point.

An hour doesn't feel very long when you want it to be. But duty back at the shop called; 1 p.m. always ushered in a rush. So I finished my scrapple, egg, and cheese on wheat at Angelo's and headed back out into the midday sun.

Only a couple of people were waiting for me when I got back—not bad for a Saturday. "Back to the salt mine," I announced, walking past them and unlocking the door. I held the door for them as a third person pulled up and honked the car horn.

Nothing makes time fly by more quickly than a busy shop. I love helping people, and if people are willing to pay for that help, I feel like one of those lucky ones who have found jobs they are good at and truly love. I have been a loner most my life and quite happy about it; I'd rather have a small but incredibly close group of friends than be popular and socialize. But the way I feel when I solve a person's problem—the gratitude I receive when I've made someone's day better, all the positive feelings that accompany a job well done—outweighs the disdain I sometimes feel for humanity.

This behavior is not unique to me; computer technicians tend to like to fix broken things, not deal with people. They would rather be locked in a closet and told to turn screws all day than be at a service bar checking in customers, who can be messy, emotional, boring, and incredibly rude. But when you choose a career in customer service, it has to start with a positive initial customer interaction; you can't just skip to the repair. If you fail the customer from the start, then it doesn't matter if you fix the problem or not.

At 4 p.m., the shop traffic died down. All the machines needing repair had been checked in and moved through initial triage. Notes had been completed, and people who needed calling had been called. Finally, I could get back to Hunter's computer, which I figured would be charged up enough for me to take another crack at it.

I pulled the blinds and locked the door to avoid any more interruptions, then grabbed an Amstel Light from the fridge and planted myself in front of the recovery Mac.

Here's where things started to get interesting.

The previous recovered window was open on the left, and I was waiting for the hundreds of files on the original to populate to the right. Scrolling down, I started to see files that didn't align. I started to individually drag and drop the files to the recovery folder. It took only a few files before I noticed pornography appearing in the right column.

This is a vocational hazard; I'd gotten rather used to and gave it no mind. I was a little amazed by the sheer quantity though, and by the boldness of leaving porn files on one's desktop. Again, it was nothing I hadn't seen before, so I kept dragging and dropping. It generally is well-known what people do on and with their computers. The industry as a whole tries not to think about gross. But I was hired to do a job, and I was going to do it.

"Oh shit," I thought, pausing. The preview image in the right column was clearly displaying the customer. He was wrapped in a rainbow boa and wearing what looked like a jock strap. I couldn't help but chuckle.

"How embarrassing!" I thought. "Who on God's earth would feel comfortable with this lying around on their desktop?"

But I shook it off and continued down the list of files. It didn't take long before another one appeared, and then another. Hunter, with his salt-and-pepper stubble, stared into the camera attempting to look cool while taking a naked selfie. Gross.

"How many of these does he have?" I wondered. It wasn't just him alone either. Although it looked like he was having a love affair with himself, there also were photos with women. I decided I'd had enough, that I was no longer going to preview the data. I would just go by the file name and hope for the best. And I tried to work out how to keep a straight face when he returned for the recovery data.

I continued copying files until I got to one titled "income.pdf." I likely wouldn't even have noticed it if it hadn't been tagged with a purple dot. On a Mac, you can apply tags, or color codes, to files as an organizational aid. It seemed odd that someone who clearly had zero organizational skills would bother tagging this one file purple. It was begging to be clicked open. So I did.

It was an email from January 16, 2017, saved as a PDF. At the top were the years 2013, 2014, and 2015. Next to each year was the amount of taxable income earned: $833,000+ in 2013, $847,000+ amended to $1,247,000+ in 2014, $2,478,000+ in 2015. I was blown away. All that money and this asshole couldn't spring for a backup drive!

I read on. Amounts that I could never even have imagined earning were broken down by the year. Then I read, "Since you couldn't have lived on $550,000 a year, you 'borrowed' some money from RSB in advance of payments." I was speechless. This guy couldn't live on more than ten times what I earned every year?

The whole document seemed shady. I saw that a lot of money had exchanged hands, and it didn't seem like it had been recorded lawfully. But what did I know? Plus, it was none of my business. It wasn't my job to judge—just to transfer and verify. So I kept transferring data until I hit a rather large file. The file was about half transferred when the screen went blank. Dammit, the battery had run out.

I decided to call it a night and go home to rest my eyes. About a hundred gigabytes were left to go, and I felt confident that I could knock it out the next day, Sunday. I let the MacBook charge overnight and went home—but not before thoroughly washing my hands.

APRIL 14, 2019

I love sleeping in, and Sundays are usually the one day of the week when there is really no pressure to get up. Even my cats know better than to bother me before 11 a.m. It's the one day I have completely to myself. It is also the only day I get to work in the shop with no customer interactions and no interruptions.

I made my way back to the shop late in the afternoon. It was quiet and the parking lot was empty. I unlocked the door and started to open the blinds, but then I remembered the sensitive photos and information I'd seen on Hunter's computer, and locked the door behind me. I headed to the back and reluctantly picked up where I left off.

My eighty-five-dollar service fee didn't seem worth it, given what I had to look at, but I'd already agreed to take on the job. I started copying the large video file and continued transferring the smaller subfolders. An hour later, the transfers were complete and I sat back down preparing to verify the files that had been transferred. First up: the large video file. Video files are a great way to check for corruption in data transfers, as videos get distorted if the file is corrupt.

Unfortunately for me, the video was free of corruption—of the digital kind. I suddenly felt like someone driving really slowly past a terrible accident, the kind you just can't look away from even though you want to.

In the video, Hunter was performing a sex act while filming himself *and* lighting and hitting a crack pipe at the same time.

I was amazed by how he was able to pull it off, but more important, it was highly embarrassing. This was the son of the former vice president of the United States. The hairs on my neck stood up.

The video was incriminating and embarrassing—not to mention careless. I grew up in a military family, and my mother had put the fear of God into me not to do anything that would have a negative impact on my father and his career, especially as he moved up in rank. Apparently, Hunter had never had that kind of conversation with a parent.

"What a shit show," I thought. "Thank God this guy's father is no longer in office."

April 15, 2019

Monday came and went without much excitement. I called Hunter about midday and left a message requesting that he drop off a five-hundred-gigabyte external drive so I could transfer his data from the server, and told him to allow twenty-four hours for the transfer to complete. I hung up the phone and felt relieved that this repair was coming to an end.

I also felt relieved that although there had been whispers of Joe Biden's returning to politics, he probably was too old to run for president. The packed field of contenders seemed vicious, and I didn't feel like Joe had any fight left.

I have no love for career politicians, by the way. I have watched them wage war and step all over the Constitution in an effort to further their personal gain at the expense of the people they're supposed to represent. Someone is born into the right family, joins the military because it looks good on paper and not because they want to serve their country, and then cheats and steals their way to the top. The Bidens, like many political families, seemed drunk on power, with politics as the greatest source of it.

But the real reason I wanted Joe not to run? The unwanted attention I might garner for knowing what I now knew, what I had seen on his son's computer.

April 16, 2019

It's like the entire world needs their Macs fixed on Tuesdays. The work usually is nonstop, and the day goes by rather quickly. Today was no different, starting with the small line of people waiting for my arrival in the morning, then moving on to the small crowd that poured in right before my 2 p.m. lunch, and ending with the rush after the official closing time of 5 p.m.

I don't mind working after hours. If anything, I look forward to the peace and quiet of the empty store. I can spread out and work on multiple repairs without fear of being pulled away to cater to any customers. Usually. But on this evening, Hunter Biden returned with an external USB drive to hold the transferred data.

"Will this do?" he asked in his high-pitched voice, dumping out the shopping bag with the drive on the counter. He seemed drunk again.

"So I'll start the copy tonight and give you a ring in the morning when it's ready," I told him, consciously preventing my distaste from showing on my face.

"Can you send me a bill online?" he asked. I said sure.

He acknowledged that and stumbled to the door. He seemed about as drunk as before but a little more jittery and anxious. The conversation had been quick and his responses short, as if he had somewhere to be in a hurry.

At 7 p.m., I locked up the shop and pulled the blinds. I grabbed the USB drive from the counter, plugged it into the recovery server, and started the transfer. "Seven hours remaining" the notification said. Fantastic. I could run home, relax, rest my eyes, and then return to the shop to knock out repairs from 8 to 11 p.m. I could then keep an eye on the transfer so there wouldn't be any surprises in the morning.

I had an overwhelming urge to rid myself of the repair, and was willing to sacrifice sleep to do so.

APRIL 17, 2019

I arrived in the shop Wednesday morning about fifteen minutes early and headed straight to the back. The data transfer from Hunter's laptop was complete. Finally. The file count matched, and while the size of the data wasn't an exact match, that was typical and it was pretty close.

I left Hunter a message saying that the repair was complete and the computer was ready for pickup. Then I logged into Square, an online payment processor, and generated an invoice for eighty-five dollars. The repair was listed as data recovery from a liquid-damaged Mac.

I sent the invoice and neatly placed the external drive and damaged MacBook Pro in the locked customer storage area at the back of the stockroom, where it would be secure until being picked up.

Hunter didn't show up. I checked the Square invoice online, and it hadn't been paid. I waited until a little past 7 p.m. before calling it a day, sure he would be in the next day. Maybe he just had to sleep off that last night of drinking.

APRIL 18-24, 2019

Over the next few days, I began to forget more and more about the small laptop sitting on the shelf, and about its careless owner who hadn't yet collected it. It isn't hard to lose track of a repair. As more and more new repairs are checked in, previous ones are slowly pushed down the queue that shows up in my CRM, and eventually move down so far that they no longer appear in the window that fits on the screen.

Also, a torrent of stressed-out college kids quickly approaching finals week descended, expecting repairs to be done yesterday. So it was a busy week, followed by a busy weekend, quickly passing to another busy week.

A brief aside about politics here. I have generally tried to steer clear of it, and have often found myself in relationships where having similar political beliefs means more to my girlfriends than to me. Political beliefs are not what attracts me to people or what I value—or even deem important. I believe in the basics of trust, loyalty, compassion, and caring, as well as not being hateful, curt, inconsiderate, or prejudiced. In relationships, I want to focus on what we have in common and pay attention to differences only if we can learn and grow from them. Unfortunately, politics has woven itself so deeply into so many aspects of people's lives that it has become impossible to differentiate the individual threads of who they are. Everything has become black and white: "You're with me or against me." This polarization is at the root of our divided nation, I believe.

Regardless of how many Fridays I've spent dancing with my gay friends or how many gay weddings I've attended, the second someone hears that I'm conservative, I run the risk of being labeled homophobic, racist, or xenophobic. I spent a decade proving to my community that I respect and value all of its members, whether through my business or my social contributions to the art scene (I had a studio at the Delaware Center for Contemporary Arts for nearly eighteen years that was open to the public, and I participated in many events). In short, I had worked hard to earn their respect and acceptance. But Wilmington is a liberal city, and many customers have no problem coming into the shop to vent about something they've seen on the news. Just as with a repair, if someone says something I disagree with, I'll just let it go. People's political and other opinions and comments have no effect on the job I have to do.

Rather, they *didn't* have any effect until the Thursday a week after I salvaged Hunter Biden's data.

APRIL 25, 2019

"What do you think about Joe throwing his hat in the ring?" the customer asked, breaking the five-minute diagnostic silence at the bar in my shop. Joseph Biden had just released a video that day announcing his candidacy in the 2020 Democratic presidential primaries.

"Hmm," I answered, hedging. I kept my eyes on the computer screen's little blue scan-status bar as it crawled from left to right. His comment sent my mind again to Hunter's laptop and its contents, and to the increasing urgency in getting it out of my shop. The device contained incriminating files, photos, and video footage of a man whose father had just become a presidential candidate—a candidate who had been the vice president under the most popular liberal president in our history, Barack Obama.

The gravity of what I had in my possession was rapidly sinking in.

Now, if I were ever to run for president, or even consider running, I would make sure someone on my staff was responsible for all my family's electronic devices. This person would lock down these devices and make sure they would contain nothing that could jeopardize the campaign. And if I had a reckless, drug-using son, his devices and communications would be handled even more meticulously. But apparently Joe and his campaign staff didn't feel the same way.

Even worse, my name was on the signed work authorization allowing me access to the contents of Hunter's devices. Maybe he had discarded the paper on the floor of his truck or thrown it in the trash, but I'd also left a message on his cell phone and emailed an invoice—both clearly explaining that I had access to all of his personal data on the computer I'd worked on. I could easily land on the radar of anyone looking to protect him and Biden's chances of becoming the country's next president.

"The scan is complete and there were some issues, but they've been resolved," I told the customer, looking up from the screen. The test actually had finished a few minutes earlier, but I needed the extra time to get my mind back on track. "Keep an eye on it. If it acts up again, it might be time for a new drive," I added, powering down the Mac and sliding it across the bar.

Other customers came and went throughout the day. When the shop was finally empty again, I sat down and tried to focus on the repairs at hand. Burying myself in my work has always been the best way to clear my mind. From an early age, I've been able to tune out my surroundings and focus on what's in front of me, if it holds my interest. And I truly loved working on Macs. I had a knack for it, even with my visual disability, and doing repairs was rewarding—as was owning a successful business in an area that someone had told me I couldn't be successful in. The feeling of silently proving people wrong was just as rewarding as announcing a successful repair. Because of all those things, I had no problem putting on blinders and focusing solely on my work.

Usually. Tonight, I had a hard time focusing.

"This is ridiculous," I told myself, frustrated. "Joe Biden has been involved in politics for almost half a century. He and his family should be pros at damage control and would have thought of everything. You can't run around in your underwear smoking crack, and film it no less, unless you know how to keep it completely hidden from the public."

And yet...

Maybe the family and staff didn't know about Hunter's behavior. Maybe they saw only the well-groomed, clean-cut son of a statesman. Maybe if they knew what he was really like and what he'd been doing, they'd never even have let him out of the house, let alone be allowed to hand incriminating personal devices over to complete strangers.

Then again...

There was no way that any family or staff member in their right mind would leave damning evidence like this unattended. If I were on anyone's radar, it would be because the whole thing was being well-handled, and I'd be protected.

My mind ran back and forth between these two scenarios, finally landing on the side of feeling comforted that someone had been paying attention to Hunter's behavior and was handling things. That I'd be fine.

My focus returned, and I continued working. Next on the agenda: calling all of the customers who still hadn't picked up their repairs, as was customary at the end of each month in an effort to get invoices paid in a timely manner. I started down the list, calling customers and leaving messages. It was only after the phone started ringing that I realized I had dialed Hunter's number.

I prayed to be taken to voicemail.

My voice sounded crackly and weak as I left a message. I wasn't even sure what I said made sense, as I was way overthinking the situation. When I hung up the phone, I sat there for a minute, reflecting on what a horrible spy I'd make.

★ ⚑ ★

At home that evening, I kept turning everything over in my mind: the anxiety, the phone call, the incriminating things I'd seen, the fear gnawing at my gut. I couldn't put my finger on exactly why I was afraid, but my gut made it clear I was.

I knew very little about Hunter. In fact, I knew more of his deceased brother, Beau Biden. He'd seemed like a good guy, loved and respected in the community. His future had seemed bright. And I knew that his and Hunter's mother and sister had died in a car crash when the boys were very young. I couldn't imagine the loss they must have felt, nor the pressure in having a father like Joe. I decided to do a little research on the family to gain some understanding and hopefully ease my worry.

I typed "Hunter Biden" into my web browser's search field and clicked the Wikipedia link. Hunter had been in the Navy? Oh, the Navy reserves. But not for long; apparently he'd been kicked out for cocaine use. He'd received a special waiver for age, joining when he was forty-three.

I didn't know you could even join the military at that age. I quickly revisited my youth and remembered what I would have given to join the military. Both of my grandfathers had been pilots, as well as my father and one of his brothers. If felt like serving in the military was the family business, and I wanted so badly to serve.

When I was seventeen, a recruiter called the house.

"He's blind and can't join," my mother yelled in frustration. I got the feeling this wasn't the first call she had received.

I wondered now if maybe my family had been wealthy or powerful enough, they could have gotten me into the military. Hunter's father had administered his commissioning oath at the White House. I guess that's how powerful you need to be. Hunter had been a direct commissioned officer, which means he didn't have to go through an academy or any other form of officer training. He'd been handed a commission at the White House by his dad, the vice president.

Along with the waiver for age, Hunter had received a waiver for a past drug-related incident. I started to see a trend. I read further. He'd had a relationship with his deceased brother's widow, Hallie Biden, whom I recognized as a star in Hunter's porn videos. A picture quickly grew of a man who had struggled for decades with drug use, but at the same time had taken full advantage of the wealth and power his family provided.

My searching also showed a family complicit in Hunter's actions and behavior, while still providing support and opportunities well beyond what an average person could ever imagine. How could the family not know about the unsavory details of Hunter's personal life? They were all over the internet. Granted, he was portrayed as the victim in most cases: enduring a lifelong struggle to deal with loss, experiencing the accompanying momentary lapses of judgment.

But on his own laptop, I didn't see a victim. I saw an addict—whether his addiction was sex, drugs, or both. And I saw someone addicted to money and power, a guy who couldn't survive on over half a million a year. A guy who was careless and reckless, whose family seemed endlessly willing to help him and keep throwing opportunities at him, which he kept throwing away. My pity for this guy was fading fast, while my fear over what his family would do to keep his secrets grew.

I would do anything to protect my family. I would go to the wall for them. That's what family members do. And I assumed that other families shared this feeling. So I assumed the Biden family would do anything to protect their own.

And they were very wealthy and very powerful.

And I might be seen as a threat to their own.

MAY 2019

I was sitting in my shop on the evening of my birthday. Little had eased my thoughts about my delinquent customer, but gearing up for my birthday weekend was a welcome distraction.

"There's no way Joe is going to win the election," I thought, a few margaritas helping put my fears to rest. "I have nothing to worry about. He's too old, and nobody is going to take him seriously." I'd even heard a rumor that Barack Obama didn't want Joe to run. There were about twenty other candidates, too, most of them younger and seemingly way more popular. What was I afraid of? Nobody was going to come looking for the computer. It was on the shelf in the back collecting dust, and I decided to shelve my fears too.

Confident in my reasoning, I spent the rest of May working my tail off with few, if any, thoughts of men in black showing up at my shop. I even left another message for Hunter to collect his computer, this one sounding normal, disclosing my identity and purpose. I was quite confident I would never see Hunter again.

Mid-June, Hunter started showing up in the news.

I initially avoided reading the headlines, mainly because I didn't really care but also because I was in denial. When the name Burisma appeared in a headline next to Hunter's photo, however, I started to pay attention. I remembered the file named "income.pdf" I had opened revealing questionable financial dealings. I'd seen a note about Hunter's joining the board of Burisma in 2014 and having to amend his returns to account for an additional $400,000 that hadn't been reported. What was this guy doing on the board of a natural gas company in Ukraine? And what could he possibly have done to deserve $400,000 for it?

I took to the internet again. In my very limited research, here's what I found.

- Hunter Biden graduated with a bachelor of arts degree from Georgetown University and later got a law degree.

- He then got a position at MBMA, a Delaware bank that was a big contributor to his father's campaigns, and rose to the rank of executive vice president.

- He went off into the world of lobbying.

- He was appointed to the board of Amtrak for five years, but left shortly after his father became vice president in 2009. He was quoted as saying it was time for his lobbying activities to end.

Nothing besides maybe the Amtrak and lobbying experience seemed to have qualified him for a position on the board of Burisma. If he was lobbying, whom was he lobbying for? But more important, whom was he lobbying? My focus shifted from Hunter to Burisma and its recently revealed dealings in the news. I read about its being investigated for fraud in London in 2014, and about many other Ukrainian internal investigations. A story of a corrupt company run by some very powerful, shady people was coming together.

The more I read, the more it seemed this was the norm in Ukraine. Wealthy Ukrainian oligarchs run powerful corporations much like our own pirates of Silicone Valley do. To them, having $21 million in assets frozen is just another occupational hazard. And, of course, the Ukrainian oligarchs have their hands in politics, but they enjoy direct involvement as opposed to using lobbying puppets.

I respect the people of Ukraine. They endured Soviet rule and fought bravely for independence—and are fighting to keep it as I write this—only to trade it in for political and corporate corruption.

"Why was Hunter there?" I wondered. "What was he doing for all that money?"

Oh, I just answered that first question with the second.

If Hunter was there for the money, what exactly was Burisma paying him for? Over the next few weeks, tales of corrupt business dealings and influence-peddling surrounded the younger Biden. Meanwhile, the older Biden wasn't doing so well on the election trail, unsurprisingly.

So far, my reasoning was holding true: He was not a serious contender for the White House; therefore, I wasn't a threat to him. My fears related to what I was sitting on evaporated.

Almost.

But I was also curious. I learned that Rudy Giuliani, former attorney and mayor of New York City, was in Ukraine, researching possible Ukrainian interference during the 2016 election as well as a pay-for-play scheme conducted by the former administration. I knew I was in possession of embarrassing and incriminating information, but could what I'd seen be considered criminal? Was Hunter's laptop the missing piece in an ongoing criminal investigation?

And what would happen to my business and my social life if I got caught handing it over to the authorities? On the other hand, what might happen if I concealed the evidence and didn't report it? There seemed no easy answer to these new questions. I chose to keep an eye on the news and wait. I still didn't even understand what I had seen, what it was exactly. And the possible repercussions of my turning over the laptop to the authorities seemed to outweigh any moral obligation to do so since I didn't even know yet what was the right thing to do.

Over the next few weeks, when something in the news about Burisma or Hunter caught my eye, I investigated it. This research was just an armchair pastime at this point. I took very crude notes, mainly names and dates. For the most part, my real life was pretty busy, so I didn't have time to play detective. I had discovered a passion for woodworking and had not been devoting my free time to much else.

In the spring, as a way to get back in the creative saddle, I had built my own CNC machine for woodworking projects. For the first time, I could create an image on the Mac and transfer it to a wooden medium. My first real project was to replicate the cockpit structure of a North American P-51C Mustang, a single-seat fighter plane used in World War II and the Korean War.

It was a good project, and I was happy to be creating again. And, as with most things I develop a passion for, this one consumed all my free time. So I didn't even notice when the ninety-day period for a checked-in device to be considered an abandoned product came and went for Hunter's computer. It all seemed part of the forgotten past.

Then came the *Washington Post* article.

July 2019

The *Washington Post* ran an article on July 22 titled "As vice president, Biden said Ukraine should increase gas production. Then his son got a job with a Ukrainian gas company."[1] It sparked a connection in my mind and answered some lingering questions I'd had.

I did a little digging and figured out that Joe Biden had been tapped as a point man for the Obama administration on all things Ukraine a few weeks before Hunter was appointed to the Burisma board. Joe had been having geopolitical discussions about increasing gas production, and within a few weeks, his son was taking money from a Ukrainian natural gas company. At the very least, this screamed nepotism; at its worst, it was illegal. Was a pay-for-play grift being run out of the White House? Could the answer to that be hidden on the laptop that was now legally my property? There was only one way to find out, and curiosity got the better of me.

You know what they say about curiosity.

I had not viewed the contents of Hunter's laptop since mid-April. It had been three months, with a fair amount of stress over it during that time, and I was determined to not revisit my fears. I decided to clone the copy of his computer's drive that I'd already created to another Mac with internet access disabled. That way I could look at the contents as if they were on Hunter's Mac, but without the risk of any syncing with the cloud, which could prevent the access of cached emails and messages.

My PC-using friends have always admired the ease with which Macs back up and restore customer data. On a Mac, the way I prefer to restore data to a new drive—or in my case, a different machine—is simple and effective: installing an operating system to the newly formatted drive. If you do it right, everything will look and operate exactly as it did the last time the machine was on.

It worked perfectly, and I now had an exact clone of Hunter's drive on my Mac. Now I just needed another Mac for all my notes and with the ability to connect to the internet for research. Armed with my project, I locked up the shop and headed home.

It's only a block and a half up Delaware Avenue to my house, but that night I opted for a longer and more secluded route: two blocks up Gilpin Avenue and down Scott Street.

My house is a 1920s townhome and a labor of love. I purchased it for a great price in 2014, mostly because of its condition. The field stone basement leaked like a sieve. It had been a frat house in a former life, and the beer-stained wood floors told the story. The yellowed and cracked plaster walls showed its age. Oh, and the kitchen was a perfect time capsule from 1981, just with a lot more rust and wear. But I saw the home's potential, and it was livable.

Slowly, I gave the home new life. It's still a work in progress, but I love it. It has a brick face trimmed in white and forest green. An American flag flies from the corner of the covered porch. Above the awning on the second floor, being true to my Scottish roots, I usually fly the flag of Nova Scotia and/or Scotland. When you walk in, you're greeted with a dark green living room with white crown molding. On every wall are gilded, framed paintings. A lovely little crystal chandelier hangs in front of a large iron-framed rectangular mirror. A large oval wooden coffee table is surrounded on three sides by claw-footed turn-of-the-previous-century couches and loveseats.

A large sixty-inch flat-screen TV occupies the space where a recessed bookshelf once stood. I usually sit on the loveseat, right in front of the TV. From about two feet, I can see it pretty well, but I still need a little help with captions and subtitles. Tonight I grabbed an end table from the basement and positioned it in front of the loveseat. On it, I placed both Mac notebooks side by side, and ran their power cords to the outlet behind the seat. Alone and ready, I opened an Amstel Light and powered on the devices.

"What's up, buddy?" asked a familiar voice behind me.

Oh shit. I didn't think my best friend Chip was coming over tonight.

"Oh, not much," I answered. "Just bringing a little work home with me."

Chip and I had met around 2000 at Ameristar Technologies, a pretty successful systems integrator that had hired me from the Delaware Department of Education to be its lead Apple service tech for its collection of Fortune 500 companies. Chip had been a sales rep. We'd met through a coworker, and a friendship had grown quickly around waterskiing, drinking beer, and eating crabs.

When Ameristar began downsizing as the dot-com bubble burst, Chip, myself, and two-thirds of the company were let go. But we had developed a bond and decided to stick together. And when the shop was doing well enough for me to buy a house, Chip moved some of his stuff in. It was a big house, so I didn't mind. Plus, he already had an apartment and a four-thousand-foot warehouse on top of that, and spent most of his time elsewhere. He would just come hang out on the weekends and enjoy the Trolley Square nightlife. I guess tonight was one of those nights.

I knew I had to tell Chip what I was up to with Hunter's laptop. It was only fair. If I was bringing danger into the house, he had a right to know. Maybe I could be vague and just say that I'd done a data recovery job and the laptop had been abandoned. He didn't need to know who…

"Holy shit, is that Hunter Biden?" Chip blurted.

The Mac had just booted up, and the system had restored itself to its previous state. Anything that had been open the last time Hunter had used the Mac had automatically reopened. I guess he had been looking at his homemade porn collection before the spill that had brought him to my shop.

"What the hell are you doing with that?" Chip asked.

Well, shit. So much for my secret-keeping ability. I told Chip everything, explaining that I wanted to see if anything on the laptop could fill in the missing pieces from what we had seen on the news.

He shared my fears of retaliation from the Bidens over what was on the laptop and what I had seen. He was quick to express his discomfort.

"Do you have to do this here? Can't you do that at the shop?" he pleaded.

I understood his concerns. He was a father and I wasn't. He had his girls to think about, and disapproved of anything that might jeopardize his ability to be with them. I assured him I had taken steps to ensure that nothing would be hackable with the device's Wi-Fi card removed.

"Well, I don't want to hear about it," Chip said, reluctantly. "And I don't want to talk about it."

With that awkward conversation behind us, I turned to the booted-up Macs.

How could Hunter have found anything he needed on that desktop? It looked like a digital dumping ground.

Ignoring the sea of porn, I went straight for Burisma. I did some basic computer-wide searches on the company, which brought up mostly pay stubs as recent as February 2019 and a couple of signed board member documents.

The pay stubs were mind-boggling. Thirty-six thousand dollars a month! This guy has been making $36,000 a month for almost five years. Plus, there was a $2 million initial Burisma payment shown in the document I'd discovered during the transfer. Again, I wondered: What was this guy doing that was worth that kind of money?

I was determined to figure it out, and I knew the answers were hiding right in front of me.

For the next month, I dove into the laptop every evening. I searched emails and files, matching places and names with dates and times. I built a timeline of events that painted a dark picture of corruption and abuse of power.

The subjects of that picture? A small group of men trying to grab a large amount of money.

PART TWO

THE THREATS

THE BURISMA GRIFT: 2014-2016

The following information comes from my media research and what I found, including copies of emails, on Hunter's computer.

It all started on February 20, 2014, when Russia invaded Ukraine. The next day, the pro-Russian Ukraine president, Viktor Yanukovych, fled Ukraine with Russia's assistance. This guy seemed about as corrupt as they come.

To help stabilize the region, the International Monetary Fund (IMF) put together a $17.5 billion loan that would be released over the next four years. On March 11, the IMF approved the loan; two days later, the first $5 billion was released to Ukraine and distributed to the energy sector, mainly natural gas providers. The idea was to undercut the bulk of natural gas being imported by Russia into Ukraine by offsetting the price of natural gas.

Burisma, being Ukraine's largest provider of natural gas, gladly took the money.

There was one condition: The fund demanded that Ukraine establish an anticorruption bureau to root out corruption and oversee the distribution of the funds. Unfortunately, less than two weeks later, on March 26, the interim government announced that natural gas prices would rise by 50 percent.

What happened to the money the IMF gave Burisma to prevent this level of inflation? Around that time, two guys halfway around the world were asking that very question.

At 12:43 a.m. on April 13, 2014, Hunter sent his friend Devon Archer an email detailing exactly how they were going to take advantage of what was happening in Ukraine. In their exchange, they predicted the election of Petro Poroshenko, a true reformer by Ukrainian standards, as president. With his election, Burisma would be pushed to honor the IMF loan and lower gas prices. The two friends saw this as an opportunity to step in and aid Burisma. They clearly understood what Burisma had done with the money, and saw a way to cash in.

If the U.S. government could step in and place more sanctions on Russia, that would drive the price of Russian gas up even more, giving Burisma the chance to step in and finally lower its gas prices enough to look like a national hero while still profiting greatly off the IMF loan. They saw Vice President Joe Biden, referred to by Hunter as "my guy," being the public face for the administration and its handling of Ukraine. They saw the opportunity that U.S. backing would bring and positioned it as a selling point to Burisma.

Announcing a trip to Ukraine by the vice president of the United States would restore the IMF's faith in Ukraine and place pressure on Russia, taking the focus off Burisma.

Hunter and Devon planned for a long-term agreement and across-the-board participation. They knew the venture would be risky in the short term, given all the directions that elections and invasions can go in. But Devon and Hunter figured that successfully leveraging the influence they now peddled could be invaluable in expanding Burisma's operations outside Ukraine; after all, they did have other domestic and foreign partnerships in China, Mexico, Black Sea countries, and Poland.

The two discussed creating a corporate entity separate from their other ventures. They saw the money-making potential but also the need for secrecy. They didn't want to get greedy and have their other ventures suffer, so they worked out a plan for minimal involvement in those ventures. They talked about getting burner phones from a 7-Eleven convenience store.

They were looking to get some money up front from Burisma to give them capital for this new entity. Apparently, the money they were expecting to get from China wasn't coming in, so they needed cash to get everything started. They also wanted to find a highly credible and discreet firm to perform due diligence and deep information searches on an ongoing basis. They were looking for the kind of people who could get them information that wasn't available through a Google search and some phone calls.

They would use their own personal funds to pay for it. Hunter told Devon, "I'm sure your buddies down in Little Creek have some trusted independent contacts that do that sort of work." Little Creek, Virginia, is home to the Joint Expeditionary Base, the major operating base for the amphibious forces of the U.S. Navy's Atlantic Fleet.

Armed with a plan, they set out to make their pitch to Burisma, hoping a visit to Ukraine by Hunter's father would be enough to get their foot in the door. Apparently, it was.

On April 16, 2014, Vice President Joe Biden met with Devon Archer at the White House. Five days later, the VP traveled to Ukraine to personally show the support of the administration for the natural gas sector.

The day after that, Devon was awarded a position on Burisma's board of directors. And a little less than three weeks later, on May 12, Hunter joined him on the board, to the tune of $1,295,000 each.

The day Hunter joined the board, he and Devon received an email from Vadym Pozharskyi, Burisma's number-two guy, asking for help. Burisma was and still is owned by Mykola Zlochevsky, a Ukrainian politician and oligarch who has amassed wealth and power in both private and public life. He has been and continues to be at the heart of many investigations of corruption both within and outside Ukraine.

Vadym was Mykola's right-hand man, his protégé, and was Mykola's voice when speaking to Hunter and Devon. In the email, Vadym explained that on a number of occasions, the representatives of new authorities in power had tended to be quietly aggressive, approaching Mykola unofficially with the aim of obtaining cash from him.

Initially, representatives of the ultranationalist political party Svoboda and the Ukrainian Ministry of Internal Affairs were making the requests; these so-called unofficial communications would entail blackmail if Mykola didn't cooperate. Vadym went on to explain that after unsuccessful attempts to receive funds from Mykola, the ministry began to formally investigate Burisma and its dealings.

This investigation led to the intimidation of Burisma's clients, partners, and suppliers in the ministry's effort to get them to stop doing business with Burisma. This is a typical method of disabling businesses in Ukraine.

Then Vadym asked Hunter and Devon for help. "We urgently need your advice on how you could use your influence to convey a message/signal, etc, to stop what we consider to be politically motivated actions," he wrote. Vadym wanted the U.S. government to press the Ukrainian government to take the pressure off Mykola, and now with Hunter on the board, that could happen.

In an internal response from Hunter to Devon concerning the request, it was stressed that they needed a lobbyist. They wanted to avoid direct involvement to prevent having to register under the U.S. Lobbying Disclosure Act and the Foreign Agents Registration Act. Basically, a middleman was needed to discreetly convey Vadym's needs to the appropriate government agencies.

Time was running out for Vadym, so he didn't waste any time cashing in on favors from his newly minted board members. And on May 25, 2014, Petro Poroshenko was elected president of Ukraine. Vowing to root out corruption, he immediately started an official investigation into Burisma as well as into Ihor Kolomoyskyi, the company's rumored silent partner.

Ihor was and is a billionaire businessman and politician—and a bad man. His strong-arm tactics and questionable/illegal financial dealings have earned him a spot on Russia's most-wanted list. He was believed to be supported by a security team of ex-Mossad (Israeli national intelligence agency) agents, and his favorite tool for negotiation was rumored to be a hatchet. Not someone you would want to work with, let alone try to rip off.

Beginning in late May and continuing over the next few months, Hunter and Vadym visited Kazakhstan on behalf of Burisma, sans Secret Service agents. In addition to perks like visas, policies, and internal documents pertaining to the Ukraine, Vadym was provided protection by the U.S. government from the Ukrainian government. Vadym got what he wanted out of the access the two men provided, and they each got about $50,000 a month in return as compensation for being on the board.

Fast-forward to November 2014, when things started to get more complicated.

Mykola transferred $24 million to a Latvian branch of PrivatBank, a Ukrainian bank owned by Ihor Kolomoyskyi. In December, Mykola got caught paying $7 million in bribes to officials serving under Ukraine's prosecutor general, in an effort to shut down that office's investigation. Mykola then fled Ukraine amid allegations of unlawful self-enrichment and legalization of funds during his tenure in public office.

On February 5, 2015, Vadym again emailed Hunter and Devon, saying he needed their advice on an important issue:

> The thing is, when a Ukrainian citizen goes to Mexico, he or she applies for a Mexican visa online and within a week gets the visa in a form of an

electronic voucher. When he or she flies to Mexico, the customs officers at the airport verify its validity and grant entry. However, today I was notified by our travel agent about the following situation: a person's American visa has been revoked due to unknown reasons, she applied for a Mexican visa, received it without any problems, flew with her family all the way to Mexico to celebrate the New year and on the border to Mexico was denied entry on the grounds that she some issues with the American embassy and supposedly Mexico and the USA customs authorities share the same database. As a result, she got back to Kyiv on the plane. So my query is obvious, since Mykola also had some issues and his visa was revoked and he hasn't applied for a new one. With this in mind, I feel that there's a risk that he will fly to Mexico and would be denied entry, and in bad mood would be forced to come back. Please advise here.

Hunter and Devon were quick to provide contacts at the State Department and grease the wheels for Mykola's visa.

Those connections soon would come in handy for Ihor as well.

On March 25, 2015, President Poroshenko signed a decree dismissing Ihor from his post as head of Dnipropetrovsk RSA, the region's local government. Soon after, Ihor obtained a U.S. visa and started visiting the United States while residing mainly in Switzerland.

Oligarchs were not the only ones taking interest-ing flights abroad. On April 17, Vadym thanked Hunter for the opportunity to meet his father. Then on July 23, Vadym emailed Hunter about his and his family's August trip to Paris from Washington, D.C., as there seemed to be some confusion over the children's passports with the Secret Service. Then on August 2, Hunter and the Secret Service traveled to Paris on Vadym's dime. The Secret Service stayed in Paris as Hunter and Vadym continued to travel to Romania on a private jet.

After a few days, they returned to Paris and headed back to D.C. It would seem things were going great for Hunter and Devon. The two had proven themselves useful to their powerful Ukrainian overlords and were being rewarded well—so well that they were able to hire a company to perform the heavy lifting between Burisma and the White House. They chose Blue Star Strategies, a self-described "dynamic, bipartisan interdisciplinary government rela-tions and public affairs consultancy based in Washington, D.C. with offices in Europe and Latin America serving global clients." In this case, Blue Star ended up providing a private Ukrainian gas company with vital information directly from the executive branch of the U.S. government.

Blue Star was brought on board on November 24, 2015, and by December 2 was providing weekly reports from the White House based on agendas and documents related to the administration's policies toward Ukraine. Why was this intel coming from the executive branch of the White House and not the office of the vice president, who was supposedly in charge of Ukraine affairs? If Blue Star was working for Burisma, and this sensitive data was coming directly from the executive branch, that could mean Obama was the one really calling the shots in Ukraine and Joe Biden was just the "bag man."

I wondered who else at the White House could be using Blue Star in a similar fashion. Along with that weekly report at the time was the vice president's detailed schedule for his upcoming trip to Ukraine. Normally a national security secret, this information was being sent over unsecured email to an address belonging to a private Ukrainian citizen.

In other words, Blue Star was sending classified information to a nonsecure foreign source.

This increased connectivity and access was vital now, as the anticorruption government of Ukraine was pressing harder on Mykola and Burisma through ongoing investigations. Luckily for the latter two, on December 8, 2015, Vice President Biden visited Kiev and threatened to withhold *$1 billion* in loan guarantees unless Ukraine's top prosecutor, Viktor Shokin—who was investigating Burisma—was fired. And guess what? Shokin was fired soon after. Devon and Hunter had saved the day.

So for the moment, the pressure was off and it looked like smooth sailing for Burisma and the gang. But all good things come to an end.

★ ⚑ ★

When Donald Trump won the 2016 U.S. presidential election, Burisma no longer found itself under the protection of the White House. It didn't take long for the Ukrainian government to quickly change its tune from being submissive to the U.S. government's pressure to drop the investigation into Burisma to launching an all-out war on the corrupt oligarchs. On December 18, 2016, after a two-year investigation, it nationalized PrivatBank. Ihor Kolomoyskyi, the principal owner, fled to Israel but maintained ownership of his eighteen shell companies based in the American state of Delaware, all started between late 2008 and 2016. And, just as it did when handing out visas to Vadym Pozharskyi and others, the State Department turned a blind eye.

Those eighteen shell companies were most likely used to launder the $5.5 billion that Ihor embezzled from PrivatBank before it was nationalized. In a bizarre twist, while in exile, Ihor promoted a TV star on a station he owned and funded the actor-comedian's presidential campaign.

That man, Volodymyr Zelensky, went on to become the sixth president of Ukraine. And what was one of his first actions as president? Declaring the nationalization of PrivatBank illegal, thereby absolving Ihor from any wrongdoing and allowing him to return to Ukraine. Needless to say, Burisma was off the hook as well. I guess if you can't beat them, build yourself a president and defeat them.

By mid-2016, Devon seemed to have had enough and left the board. Hunter, on the other hand, continued to collect $36,000 a month until his contract ended in April 2019. And at his request, a board position was granted to Joseph Cofer Black, who'd been a CIA officer and served as director of the Counterterrorism Center under George W. Bush. In 2005, after leaving the CIA, he joined private security company Blackwater (later renamed Xe Services and now called Academi) as vice chairman.

He stayed there for a couple of years and later assisted former Massachusetts governor Mitt Romney with counterterrorism and foreign affairs during Romney's 2008 and 2012 presidential campaigns. In 2016, he was appointed to the board of Burisma, at Hunter's request. By now, it was clear that being on the board was a reward for service to the oligarchs. And what had Black done to earn his seat?

A chill ran down my spine when I remembered the email Hunter had sent Devon on April 13, 2014, when they were plotting the Burisma grift. I went back to my notes and reread it. It included Hunter's noting the need for "the kind of people that can get us information that's not available through a Google search and some phone calls. We can use our own funds to pay for it and I'm sure your buddies down in Little Creek have some trusted independent contacts that do that sort of work." Could that have been referring to the Joint Expeditionary Base–Little Creek?

I had a trusted source who might be able to shed some light on the question. My father had been an Air Force colonel for thirty-one years and also had spent some time in the CIA.

"Quick question," I said casually over the phone, trying not to raise any suspicion. "Are you familiar with Joint Expeditionary Base–Little Creek?"

"Sure, what about it?" he responded.

"Was there any relationship with the base and other agencies or branches?"

"Well, it was a joint base, so the Army trained their special forces guys there, as well as the Marines," he said. "Right around the corner at Dam Neck, SEAL Team Six did their training."

Blackwater had been started by a former Navy SEAL. I wondered if there was a connection.

"What about the agency?" I asked, referring to the CIA.

"I don't know if anyone trained there, but Camp Peary is an hour up the road."

"What was Camp Peary?" I asked, typing the same question into a Google search field.

"It's the Farm," he answered. I fell silent. That chill ran down my spine again.

The Farm was a covert facility used to train officers of the CIA's Directorate of Operations (sometimes called the Clandestine Service) just down the road from Little Creek.

"What is this all about?" he asked finally. No way was I going to tell him.

"Nothing," I said quickly. "The name came up in something that I read, and I was trying to get some information that I couldn't find in a Google search." Now realizing I

JOHN PAUL MAC ISAAC

was using my father in much the same way that Hunter could have been using Black, I said thanks and ended the call with the traditional family exchange of "cheers."

But I certainly wasn't feeling cheery.

The anxiety I'd had about being discovered with the laptop's contents returned with a vengeance. Now I recognized that the laptop posed a very real threat—to me and others—and that some very powerful players were involved, possibly including government agencies. While this had never been just a case of some random crackhead with embarrassing porn on his computer, it hadn't seemed quite this serious before.

Now I saw that this was a national security situation.

It was possible that U.S. government agencies were being manipulated to the benefit of the Biden family. I had already seen how Special Prosecutor Robert Mueller had weaponized FBI agents during his investigation into Russian interference in the 2016 U.S. presidential election, so it wasn't outside the realm of possibility that the CIA had some "bad apples" working a side hustle for the Bidens.

My fears shifted from my disappearing at the hands of some Secret Service thug to being thrown in a dark hole by the CIA. I couldn't decide which was worse. I knew I had to get the laptop to the authorities. To someone who could protect me and investigate the evidence. I had to get this equipment out of my shop and into the hands of the FBI.

EARLY SEPTEMBER 2019

I've been attending reunions of airmen who served during World War II through Vietnam for the past twenty years. I bring my camera equipment to these typically weeklong events and videotape interviews for archival and historical preservation. I call it my vacation. I get to sit around and have a few beers with some true heroes and listen to their war stories.

History might be written by whoever wins, but the truth is told by the people who fought. Even though I couldn't honor my country by serving, at least I can honor those who have by preserving their memories. I started filming in the late 1990s, captivated by the stories of airmen who'd been stranded behind enemy lines during World War II, and also of the men and women who offered them aid and shelter. I found myself chasing down these heroes each year and preserving more and more of history.

The 2019 year airmen reunion was being held in Salt Lake City, Utah. I flew out to my aunt Kathy and uncle Neil's place on September 3, then met up with my parents, who'd driven up from Albuquerque, New Mexico. The three of us would drive the rest of the way to Utah, about a seven-hour drive, in their Jeep.

I wanted to ask my father for help but didn't want to expose my family to the perceived risks. As I said earlier, a powerful family would do anything to protect their own. But now Joe Biden was leading in most of the nation's polls for the 2020 presidential election. And as his popularity grew, so did my need to seek help.

So on the long drive back from the reunion, I finally broke the silence and brought up the dreaded subject.

"So, I need your help," I told my father. "I had someone abandon a Mac a few months ago, and I think it has criminal activity on it and it may be part of an investigation."

"Why haven't you reported it to the local authorities?" my father responded.

"I don't feel comfortable approaching anyone local."

"Who is it? What did you see?" he inquired.

"It's Hunter Biden's Mac, and I saw some embarrassing and incriminating material on it." I gave him the bird's-eye overview, summarizing my fears.

In the back of the Jeep, my mother turned off her audiobook.

I told my father what I'd initially seen when I was hired to transfer the data, and how I feared for my life—that someone would come after me to keep things quiet. I told him how I'd waited until it had become my property before taking another look. I explained what I'd seen in the news about Hunter and Burisma, and how they had become the focus of my explorations. I began to rattle off names and events gleaned off the laptop's hard drive.

"Stop right there. I don't need to know the details," my father snapped. "Plausible deniability. I don't need your mother to hear it either."

He went on: "I agree we need to get this to the FBI, but not Wilmington or East Coast FBI—too many local boys with good-old-boy politics."

I agreed, and we continued to discuss the options. My father suggested that he pay the Albuquerque FBI field office a visit. A former Air Force colonel would carry more weight than a computer nerd, and Albuquerque would be far enough away from Washington, D.C., that we could find someone unbiased and not politically motivated to listen to my story.

It was decided. I would go back to Delaware, make a copy of the drive, and mail it to my father along with a copy of the signed work authorization. My father would approach the FBI and explain to them that he had a copy of Hunter's laptop and that it possessed evidence of criminal activity.

"I *think* it's criminal," I told my father.

"Smoking crack is illegal," he quickly reminded me.

After my father explained the situation, minus my involvement, he would wait and see how the FBI responded. The plan was, if he talked to an agent who was receptive and willing to provide adequate protection, he would provide the agent with a code word and my contact information. The agent would then reach out to me and provide the code word, and I would be free to explain the complete situation.

Why a code word? In case an email or other correspondence from the agent was intercepted and someone from outside the chain of command attempted to reach out to me first. No code word? No trust and no conversation.

We chose the number forty-two as our code word. My father had been the aircraft commander of Stinger 42 in Vietnam but was supposed to have been on Stinger 41. Captain Terence Courtney went down with Stinger 41 that day, keeping that old bird in the air long enough for seven of the ten men to bail out. My father never forgot that mission, and the number forty-two has held deep personal meaning for him ever since.

Besides a plan and a code word, we tried to work out all the worst-case scenarios. If the agent were to turn on my father and throw him under a bus, so to speak, my father would have plausible deniability for what was on the laptop. If a rogue agent out for political gains were to try to intercept the laptop and return it to its former owner, it would be impossible without the code word.

The first copy of the hard drive would go straight to my father. I would hold on to the second copy until the day my father approached the FBI, when I would then move Hunter's equipment out of the shop to a safe location with a trusted friend. If something should happen to me, the copy with my friend would be sent to Rudy Giuliani, President Trump's lawyer. My father and I both knew that once the FBI had been alerted, the risk factor would go up a notch.

We had to be very, very careful.

We both had faith in the rank-and-file agents of the FBI. We also both strongly felt that there were some bad apples, mostly high up in the food chain, that posed a threat. But we still had faith in the U.S. justice system and were confident we would find the right agent to talk to.

Back in Denver, my father drove me to the airport at about 5 a.m.—just the two of us. It didn't take long for my father to start talking.

"I wanted to have this conversation without your mother present," he said.

"What's up?" I responded, still groggy at this early hour.

"If nobody knows about this now, they will after we approach the FBI. This is a very serious situation, and it involves the highest levels of government. Your life will be in danger, and you will need to start to take this very seriously."

"I know," I answered sleepily.

"You don't know!" my father said, loudly and forcefully. "This isn't a game. These people are serious, and you won't see it coming. You need to be prepared and have a plan. 'I know' won't protect you—you have to act."

His kept his eyes on the road and his vehemence on the subject at hand.

"These people will do anything for money, and you are nobody," he said. "You would be easy to destroy both physically and financially. You need to be a step ahead all the way. If you get into trouble, run. I'm not worried about me. I've lived my life and been there, done that. There's little they could do to me. I know how these people operate and how little your life means to them."

"I understand," I said, not risking repeating "I know."

"This is not a game," my father stridently reiterated. "This is not a joke. You will have to keep your head on a swivel. After we reach out to the FBI, you will have to change your behavior. Try not to walk home the same way every night. Don't get into habits or patterns that could be easily anticipated. If you go out, don't go alone. Above all, don't talk to or trust anyone."

A deathly quiet settled over the car for the rest of the ride to the airport.

I trusted my father. He had spent thirty-one years in black ops and Special Forces. He had spent time at the CIA. It's why I'd approached him about this in the first place. He had experience with people trying to kill him, and he was a hell of a lot smarter than I was about all of this. Not to mention, a father should do everything to protect his children.

Back in Delaware, I wasted no time getting to work. Instead of buying external drives from a local store, where the purchase might be traced back to me, or online, which also could be traced and moreover might lead to damage in transit, I built my own.

It took about a week to collect all the pieces and clone the drive from the store's backup server. In essence, I created a copy that was as close to the original drive as possible. Getting into the spirit of things, I found an old Garfield stuffed animal my mother had given me a while back, and cut an opening in it just large enough to slide in the external drive and related cable. Then I "returned the gift" to my mother by handing the package off to UPS.

September 20, 2019

Waiting the three business days for the package to be delivered was excruciating. I worried that the drive would be lost—or worse, stolen by someone with nefarious motives.

Then the *Wall Street Journal* broke a story that took my attention off my worries. A whistleblower had gone to the newspaper with the contents of a leaked phone call on July 25 between newly elected Ukrainian president Volodymyr Zelensky and U.S. president Donald Trump. It revolved around the Obama administration's involvement in Ukraine, as well as Ukraine's involvement in the 2016 election.

I knew that President Trump's personal lawyer, Rudy Giuliani, had been in Ukraine throughout the summer of 2019, trying to get to the bottom of what had really happened during 2014 to 2016 under the former administration. Knowing what I knew, the president seemed completely within his rights to investigate the previous administration for corruption. Unfortunately, the mainstream and social media didn't see it that way. They saw Donald Trump pressuring a foreign leader to dig up dirt on a political opponent in an election year.

It seemed more necessary than ever to get the laptop in the hands of the authorities.

The left had been demanding President Trump's impeachment even before he took office, using alleged Russian interference in the 2016 election as a rallying cry. But that investigation ended without the left's getting its pound of flesh, and the leftists started searching for another excuse to impeach the president. With this story about the phone call, they had one.

It was actually Joe and Hunter Biden who should have been investigated, but as Joe was now a political opponent of the current administration, he got a pass—because any investigation into him or his family would be perceived as a political attack by the current administration. But the media was allowed to politically attack the president, and they weaponized every part of the phone call story they could.

SEPTEMBER 24, 2019

It took only four days for House Speaker Nancy Pelosi to announce the start of a formal impeachment inquiry over the Ukrainian phone call. I was feeling the squeeze to get the laptop into the hands of the FBI. There was no reason for this country to become even more divided over a phony impeachment proceeding; the nation had endured two previous impeachments in its 243-year history, and I didn't want it to endure the embarrassment of a third.

The secretly stuffed Garfield had arrived safely in Albuquerque, and now the ball was in my father's court. All I could do was wait and do a little work. I had to compose a letter to Rudy Giuliani to accompany the drive that would be sent to my trusted friend. I also was going to make a flash drive consisting of documents summarizing the Bidens' criminal activity, to include in the delivery.

We decided on Wednesday, October 9, as our D-Day—only about two weeks away. I don't have a lot of friends, which is fine. I had even fewer friends who would be politically inclined to help me. But one person stood out: Kristen. I had known Kristen ever since I moved to Wilmington back in the late '90s. We'd become good friends, and I was often a fixture at her apartment. We shared a more secluded lifestyle as well as the need for quality over quantity when it came to friendships. Her dad had been in the Navy and, like mine, instilled in her a love for her country as well as more traditionally conservative values. Our circles were small, and she didn't go out much. Plus, I felt she would be sympathetic to my situation and willing to help.

I called and asked her to come over, saying I needed her help with something. When she showed up, she immediately asked what was wrong. She always seemed to have an instinct for when something bad was going on.

I sat her down and gave her a rough overview of the situation. I brought her up to speed on our plans to approach the FBI, adding that I needed a safety net in case things went wrong.

"Should something happen to me, I will need you to hand-deliver this drive to 1251 Sixth Avenue, New York City, and only to someone representing Rudy Giuliani," I told her. I felt horrible placing someone I cared about in potential danger, but I also knew that I needed someone I could count on and trust.

She agreed to help.

I explained the next steps. After my father's visit to the FBI, she was to periodically check in on me by stopping by or phoning the shop. We would keep our personal calls and texts to a minimum, so as not to draw attention to her. If something went south, she would check with a mutual friend on my status, and if I were nowhere to be found for longer than a day, she was to drive to NYC and deliver the package. With the plan in place, I told her I would bring her the package in a few days.

But first, I had a letter to write.

October 8, 2019

My father called the next morning. His plan was to visit the FBI field office in Albuquerque around 10 a.m. the next day. From there on out, I would have to be extra careful. After his visit, people beyond those we trusted would know of the laptop's existence, introducing a whole new element of potential danger. For my safety net, I had to make sure to write Rudy Giuliani an attention-getting letter. I definitely didn't want to come off as a nutjob or conspiracy junkie. The letter would have to be clear and to the point, explaining my actions leading up to my father's FBI interaction without revealing his identity. I wanted to focus on my reasons for not trusting the FBI as well as my expectations for what could happen. More important, I wanted to let Giuliani know why, if he were reading the letter, I would need his help.

Here's what I came up with.

Rudolph Giuliani
Giuliani Security and Safety

Sir,

If you have received this letter, I am in need of your help. Last April 12, Hunter Biden came into my Mac repair shop in Wilmington, Delaware, requesting data recovery from 3 of his laptops. I was able to check in the one working Mac and accomplished a data recovery. He has failed to return to pay or collect the recovered data or his laptop. As the events of the summer unfolded, and after the shop's 90 day abandonment policy expired, I decided to poke around and look to see if there was anything topical on his drive. I discovered enough information that I no longer felt comfortable being in possession of his data and laptop. I decided that I wanted to turn over everything I have to the FBI or local police, but a major concern was what if compromised FBI or local police intercepted the data and destroyed it, preventing it from ending up in the hands of someone who can use it. I could not risk contacting anyone local so I mailed a copy of the drive out of state to a trusted person who would contact the FBI on Wednesday, October 9, and if trustworthy FBI were contacted, they were instructed to collect the laptop and data from my shop discreetly. If you are reading this letter, it means the compromised FBI has collected the laptop, data and possibly me. I have included a flash drive with some emails and files recovered from his laptop that could be useful in your investigation. If I am in the compromised FBI's custody, it means that there are still members of the FBI who are working to protect a former Vice-President and silence those who provide proof to his corruption. I need your help, not just to get out of custody, but also to bring to light what has happened. I have included a full copy of the laptop on an external drive. You will need a Mac to access it.

Thank you for your time and help.

John Paul Mac Isaac

Confident that I had covered all the bases, I printed out the letter and folded it to fit inside a five-by-seven-inch padded manila folder with the other two items. Then I waited for 7 p.m. to roll around so I could close the store and make the mile hike to Kristen's.

I took the long way to Kristen's, through a residential area. It was already dark, and I felt more comfortable walking through there than through an urban area. It had been over ten years since I'd been jumped, and since then I'd learned to pay better attention to my surroundings, look quickly over my shoulder, and stay under streetlights.

But that night, on the way to Kristen's, I wasn't taking any chances.

OCTOBER 9, 2019

I watched the time and waited all day, wondering how things were going with my father's visit to the FBI. Calling him would only have drawn attention to myself.

Finally, close to 8 p.m., he called.

I answered the phone with "sir," my usual greeting.

"That didn't go well," he said without any preamble. "Is it a good time to talk?"

Here's what my father told me.

He left the drive and the signed service order in his car's glove compartment, then walked into the FBI's field office armed with his military ID and a business card. He presented the ID and card to the receptionist, saying, "Ma'am, I've never done this before. Can I speak with an agent?"

She slid my father a form and requested he fill it out, which he didn't do. He wrote "sensitive" on it instead. After about a two-minute wait, the receptionist opened the door and gave my father directions to a small room divided by a thick plexiglass window and a counter. Small items could be passed under the counter, and a microphone and speaker allowed communication between both sides of the plexiglass.

My father sat down, and the receptionist opened a door on the other side of the plexiglass for a man holding the not-completed form. The agent sat down across from my father and asked, "Why did you refuse to fill out the form?"

"Well, sir, it's sensitive," my father said. "I didn't feel comfortable putting down information when I had no control over who would see it."

"How about you let me decide who gets to see what?" the agent responded.

My father went on to explain the events and his concerns for my safety. He mentioned that because I had seen content that was pornographic as well as geopolitically sensitive, my life could be in danger due to what people might do to make any potential public embarrassment disappear.

"So you think your son's life is in danger?" the agent asked.

"Yes," my father answered. He was growing more and more frustrated at the agent's behavior. The agent never looked my father in the eyes; he refused to look up from the form in his hands. Nor did he acknowledge the military ID my father had slid to the agent's side of the counter. My father didn't even know the agent's name.

"Do you have information on a specific threat to your son's life right now?" the agent asked.

"If there was a specific threat, I would have immediately called the police and not brought this to you," my father snapped back, no longer hiding his frustration.

"Well," the agent said, seemingly satisfied that he'd gotten a rise out of my father, "we don't get involved in state matters. This isn't a federal issue."

"He has the laptop of the son of a presidential candidate. It has a lot of bad stuff on it, and he needs your help," my father pleaded, trying to explain the gravity of the situation.

"OK, so was there child porn?" the agent asked.

"I don't think so. My son didn't go into detail. Why would you ask me that?"

"You said there was pornography," the agent answered. "What else did your son see?"

"Dealing with foreign interests, a pay-for-play scheme linked to the former administration, lots of foreign money."

The agent didn't seem interested. "How did your son come into possession of this laptop?" he asked.

"I have a contract with a date on it with Hunter Biden's signature that clearly states that property left at the shop longer than ninety days becomes my son's property," my father answered. "I can run out to the car and grab a copy of the paperwork and a copy of the drive."

"I want to see the paperwork. I don't want to touch the drive," the agent said. "Go out to your car and retrieve just the paperwork."

My father did exactly that. The agent made a copy of the paperwork and left the room for about ten minutes.

"I consulted with a regional legal officer, and he suggested you should get a lawyer," he said upon returning.

"Why?"

"You may be in possession of something you don't own."

"The signed paperwork clearly states that it is now my son's property," my father insisted. "I don't see why this is the issue preventing you from helping us!"

"You better lawyer up and don't talk to anyone about this," the agent shot back. "I don't have anything else for you, and the door is on the left." He nodded in the direction of the door.

My father sat there, disgusted, until the agent coldly reminded him where the door was. Then he got up, left the room, and made his way back down the hall into the main waiting area. Defeated, he walked out to his car and drove home.

At this point in his recounting of the events, I no longer heard any anger and frustration in his voice—only disappointment and humiliation. My father had given thirty-one years of his life to defend his country. A country where freedom and justice have been paid for with the blood of his brothers in arms. He felt betrayed by the very agencies for whom he had served and, more important, he had failed to get their protection for his son.

Neither of us knew what to think.

Maybe this was our firsthand experience with a two-tiered justice system—by which ordinary citizens get thrown the book for petty crimes (or, in our case, disrespectfully dismissed) while the rich and powerful get white-glove treatment. Maybe this was one bad agent not wanting to touch this case with a ten-foot pole. Either way, we were sure that we were now on someone's radar and were in a worse situation than before.

The Rest of October 2019

My fears of retaliation returned. I envisioned a newly elected President Biden sitting at his desk when his phone rings. "Sir, there is an FBI agent on line one with information about your son," his aide says. The eager and opportunistic FBI agent proceeds to gain favor with the freshly minted president by revealing the plot of a computer guy in possession of sensitive data concerning his son.

"How would you like me to personally handle it, Mr. President?" the agent asks, in essence tying a ribbon on his gift and securing his own bureaucratic future.

"Quietly," the president responds. A few days later, I am found in the park, a victim of a "botched robbery" while I was "taking an early-morning jog."

The next couple weeks were stressful, as you can imagine.

But they also were busy. I talked with my father infrequently, and when we did speak, the conversations were short. "Ops normal?" he would ask. "Nothing new. Everything is quiet," I would respond. Kristen would swing by the shop to check in on me, and I was grateful for that.

As the days went on, the feeling of being abandoned by the system sat at the front of my mind. I was focused on the idea that, as with so many noble professions and organizations, maybe this FBI branch just had a few bad apples. Maybe my father's interaction with the agent hadn't been the norm. I still wanted to believe the system worked and that justice existed, so I held out hope.

That hope was put to the test on October 28 when Nancy Pelosi announced the next stage in the impeachment inquiry. She said the House would vote that week on a resolution to officially authorize impeachment proceedings, including public hearings, and the release of the deposition transcripts.

I knew the lies the impeachment was being crafted around. I figured those lies were a form of projection brought on by the true guilty parties—parties who had influenced a foreign government for their own profit. I was building a new cause for my actions, one not based on self-preservation, fear of retribution, doing the right thing, or pursuing justice. This new cause was to prevent the nation's embarrassment of enduring a third impeachment.

I was sitting on evidence that could exonerate the president and justify his actions. Whether you like a person or not, everyone is entitled to a fair trial. And the only way this trial would be fair is if this laptop were to be admitted as evidence for President Trump's defense.

But how could I reach out to the Justice Department or even the White House without blowing my cover and dealing with the repercussions of my actions? I still had a business to run and a community to interact with. And I still believed in the chain of command. I believed that approaching the FBI again might be the only way to get what I had to the proper channels.

I started thinking about how I could approach the bureau locally. Even if it was risky, I had to try something. I felt like time was running out.

Then my father BCC-ed me on an unexpected email.

NOVEMBER 1, 2019

I didn't even know my father knew what "BCC" meant, let alone how to put it to use correctly. He used it in an email response to a call and a follow-up email he had received from Special Agent Joshua J. Wilson of the FBI's Baltimore/Wilmington division.

> Sir - thanks for the call.
>
> Was worried after a bad encounter with my FBI visit in ABQ.
>
> My son is John Paul Mac Isaac - goes by JP.
>
> His cell is ██████████.
>
> Data point; He is legally blind, does not drive. You will need to go to Him.
>
> Once you decide who is going to talk to Him, plz have him/her call Me First. Because of my background, there is a password I have that the Agent must have for JP to go forward - I did this because I feared for His life.
>
> V/R
>
> Col Steve Mac Isaac

████████████████████████████████████

Baltimore/Wilmington felt too close to home for a conversation started three weeks ago in New Mexico—a conversation that we thought had abruptly ended. How had this guy ended up with my father's contact information? Why, after weeks of nothing, were we being contacted out of the blue—and only four days after the speaker of the House announced the progression of the impeachment hearing? The timing felt odd, but I was also kind of relieved that someone from the FBI was reaching out.

A quick internet search revealed that Agent Wilson had made a name for himself at the bureau busting child predators. So far, he seemed like a great American. I have zero tolerance for men abusing children (or women), so if this guy was hunting them down and putting them behind bars, I instinctively trusted him. On social media, he seemed level-headed and an overall like a good guy—had a nice family, was a good father and someone proud of his career. Unlike the first agent my father had dealt with, maybe this guy was a "good cop."

I called my father and briefed him on what I'd discovered. We agreed that this was our best shot. All I had to do now was wait for Agent Wilson to call.

For the next few days, I thought a lot about what I was going to say and the direction I wanted the conversation to take. As noble as the goal was, putting an end to the fraudulent impeachment hearing would not be part of the conversation. This was still an agent out of the Wilmington office, not at the federal level, and my motives and my actions could not be portrayed as political. I would keep the conversation focused on my personal safety and the criminal activity I had evidence of. I wouldn't discuss any actions that could be perceived as an attack on Joe or his family. I would stick to the facts and leave emotions behind, and I would ignore the previous FBI agent's insinuations that I had broken the law—I would stick to my guns that I was doing the right thing.

If Agent Wilson were to ask me why I'd chosen to approach the FBI in Albuquerque, I would tell him the truth: that I was trying to maintain a low profile for fear of political repercussions in my community; and that my career military father, who was far more experienced in such matters, had advised it. I planned to leave out my fear that local authorities could be influenced by the powerful Biden family.

Above all, I had to play it cool. I was excited that this nightmare might be coming to an end, but I couldn't let that cloud my judgment and get me in trouble. I wasn't out of the woods yet.

November 4, 2019

I had been on the lookout for a call originating from a 973 area code, and that call finally came.

"Good afternoon. This is Special Agent Wilson from the FBI. Is this JP?"

I hate the name JP. I have always been proud of the name John Paul, as it's a combination of both my grandfathers' names.

"This is JP," I responded.

"I spoke with your father last Friday, and he expressed his concerns for your safety. He also gave me the code, forty-two," Agent Wilson said. "I would like to swing by your shop at some time and discuss your concerns. Are you free in the next few weeks?"

The last thing I wanted was for an FBI agent to pop into the shop. I wasn't ready for that level of public interaction. Trolley Square is a close-knit community—everyone is into everyone else's business. I feared the potential gossip.

"Can we meet at my home?" I asked, figuring that most of my neighbors would be at work and the block would be devoid of curious eyes. We agreed on a date and time, and I gave him my address. I stressed that my lunch break was from 2 to 3 p.m. and that I would prefer not to be late to the post-lunch rush.

"That shouldn't be a problem," Agent Wilson said. "You have my cell, so if you get into trouble or have to reschedule, please reach out."

I thanked him for the call and hung up.

Short and sweet. I felt good. I called my father and told him the agent seemed like a sincere guy and that I trusted him. For the first time since I had discovered the incriminating material, I had an interested contact at the proper authorities. I felt relieved, but as my father quickly reminded me, I still needed to be cautious. An FBI agent was coming to my home, and I needed to be careful.

I still needed a plan.

November 13, 2019

A breaking news headline interrupted my planning for the FBI visit.

Public impeachment hearings in the U.S. Senate's Committee on Intelligence had begun. If only the laptop could be in this committee's hands, this whole fiasco could end. That means the pressure was dialed way up. Agent Wilson would be knocking on my door in only six days. I wanted to print out all the documents and emails that were topical to the impeachment but that wouldn't give away any bias. I figured if I included the files that justified my fear of retaliation and showed a blatant pay-for-play scheme coming out of the previous White House, that would be enough to point this agent in the right direction.

These printouts were necessary in case the FBI took the laptop and let it sit in a lab for months while technicians combed its contents—all while the nation endured an impeachment. Without printouts, the evidence might arrive too late. Plus, I had already spent months collecting and organizing the data. Why not pass my work on to the FBI and spare them the time and effort?

I didn't want to print out anything pornographic, even though the porn was fueling my fear of domestic retaliation. It wouldn't be hard for agents to find it on the device if they looked. To address my fear of foreign retaliation, I printed out a few emails mentioning Ihor Kolomoyskyi. He was on the run with the lion's share of the billions embezzled from the IMF and Ukraine. He would be the most dangerous person involved if he had an axe to grind. I also included emails from Mykola Zlochevsky and Vadym Pozharskyi showing their access to high levels of the Obama administration.

On the domestic front, I included emails and texts residing on the laptop that directly related to the Biden family. They showed a frustrated Hunter telling his daughter he would never make her hand over half her income, unlike her grandpa had been doing. They showed Secret Service members trying to gain access to Hunter's hotel room after a suspected overdose. They told of how Hallie Biden, Beau's widow, had thrown Hunter's gun in a grocery store trash can, afraid of what he might do with it.

All highly embarrassing information that a presidential campaign would do anything to silence. And all information that needed to be seen and heard for justice to prevail.

And of course I included the smoking gun, the one that could put an immediate end to this bogus impeachment: the initial email outlining Devon and Hunter's plan to use Vice President Biden as the centerpiece of their plan to tap into the billions Burisma had to offer. The shady business dealings I had witnessed on the laptop, in my opinion, justified President Trump's phone call with Zelenskyy.

With the relevant documents printed and a copy of the signed work authorization at the ready, I was almost ready for the meeting with Agent Wilson. Last piece of prep: the delivery of a Wi-Fi camera. I planned to hide it in my living room in case the agent tried to pull something.

Worst-case scenario, my cold-blooded murder would be captured for posterity.

Unfortunately, the camera that arrived was larger than expected, about the size of a billiard ball, and had a nine-foot cable. I snaked the cable behind the TV and placed the camera in the corner of the shelf above, out in the open. It was the best I could do.

And I was out of time.

November 19, 2019

The day of Agent Wilson's visit, I was as nervous as a long-tailed cat in a rocking chair factory. Luckily, it was an otherwise typical Tuesday, so I was swamped at work. I left the shop early to inhale some lunch before the agent's 2 p.m. arrival at my home.

On the large wooden coffee table in the living room were laid out all the documents I planned to hand over. Agent Wilson would sit on the large white couch, facing the not-so-hidden camera, and I would sit in the loveseat facing him.

A loud knock on the door sounded at about 2:30 p.m.

Through the peephole, I saw a badge and card that read "FBI" in large black letters. "Could he be more obvious?" I thought.

I opened the door and cringed. Parked right in front of my house was the epitome of an undercover police car: a tired navy blue Ford Crown Victoria with dull silver hubcaps. It screamed "Feds." The only missing element was vests with "FBI" emblazoned on the back.

And Agent Wilson was not alone.

"JP, I'm Special Agent Wilson and this is Special Agent DeMeo. Can we come in?"

"Yes please," I quickly responded, getting out of their way and clearing them from my porch.

I shut the door behind them and then closed the second, interior door. I saw Agent DeMeo point to the camera on the shelf, and the two sat down on the loveseat.

"Not a great start," I thought, sitting on the couch facing the camera.

The two agents shifted around on the small loveseat, adjusting to their newfound proximity to each other. As Agent DeMeo struggled to position a clipboard with a yellow pad of paper on his leg, Agent Wilson began to ask questions.

"Did you see any child porn?" he asked.

"I don't think so," I answered. "I wasn't trying to look that close. There was a lot of porn, and it made me uncomfortable."

"What made you uncomfortable?" Agent Wilson continued as Agent DeMeo wrote on his yellow pad.

I explained that I feared for my safety, that retribution from actors both foreign and domestic seemed possible. I looked down at the paperwork intended for the agents.

"Do you really think the Bidens would try to kill you?" Agent Wilson asked.

"To keep quiet about what I know and what I've seen? Sure!" I exclaimed. "History is full of stories of people getting killed for a lot less."

"What is it that you think you saw?" he inquired. Now was my chance to show them what I had.

"This is information about Ihor Kolomoyskyi and Mykola Zlochevsky, and their involvement in using Hunter and Devon to protect the billions they embezzled from the IMF. I am afraid they would silence me for what I know," I explained, sliding the paperwork across the table toward the two agents. "This collection of emails shows preferred access to the State Department as well as the vice president's travel schedule, all sent to private Ukrainian citizens." I slid over another pile of paperwork. "Sure, I think that these people would do anything to guarantee my silence."

The agents glanced at the paperwork, then resumed their note-taking and questioning. "And how do you know it was Hunter?" Agent Wilson asked.

"Well, besides him providing his name and contact information, the same guy that came into my shop was the same guy that appeared in a lot of his porn."

"You don't think it could have been someone that resembled Hunter? You do have a visual impairment, correct?"

"I didn't recognize him when he first walked in, but later during the recovery process, I could clearly see it was the same guy. He matched his driver's license photo, his passport, and the countless examples of homemade porn."

"Why did you get your father involved?" Agent Wilson asked. "Have you spoken with anyone else about this? Any other government or law enforcement agencies?"

"I haven't talked to anyone. I asked for my father's help because he has some experience talking to professionals and I am worried about my actions being discovered locally," I explained. "I just want this laptop out of my shop and in the hands of the authorities. If there's criminal activity, it should be investigated. Mainly, I want to go away and not have my business ruined, nor my social standing. Any protection the FBI can afford me, even better."

"Well," Agent Wilson replied, "we would have to talk to our legal team to see if it's something we can take possession of."

My heart sank.

"As far as protection," he continued, "you have my cell phone. So if anyone representing Hunter or Hunter himself comes looking for it, return it to them and give us a call. It's getting close to 3 p.m., and we don't want to take up any more of your time."

I looked at my phone. I had five minutes to get back to the shop. The time had clearly sped by.

"Don't you want to take these with you?" I asked, in a desperate last-ditch effort.

"Is that a copy of the signed work authorization? Do you still have the original?" asked Agent Wilson as he reached out, avoiding the evidence and going straight for the signed work authorization.

"I have the original paperwork with the laptop and the drive." Why didn't they want to even touch the piles of evidence?

"We'll give you a ring in a few weeks and let you know where we stand," Agent Wilson said in closing.

We shook hands, and I followed them out the door and headed back to work.

★ ⚑ ★

Back home later that night, I couldn't shake my wonder about why the agents had showed no interest in the actual evidence. You'd think the FBI would want access to any and all incriminating evidence about anything related to the White House, whether past administrations or the present one—especially given the current presidential impeachment hearings.

Why had the Feds been interested enough to track me down and meet with me personally, but not interested in the information I had? Were their legal teams advising them to limit their involvement? Did they want plausible deniability, like my father initially had wanted?

I knew one thing for sure: I didn't feel any safer, and the laptop was still sitting on my stockroom shelf like a ticking time bomb.

December 2, 2019

About two weeks after the FBI's visit, Agent Wilson called.

"So, did anyone come in and collect the laptop yet?" he asked. I told him no.

"I spoke with our legal team, and they want us to bring one of our techs over to your shop next Monday," he continued. "We'll need a couple of hours to forensically clone the laptop."

"I thought the plan was to get everything out of my shop," I replied, trying to hide my disappointment. "If someone comes in, they'll know what I saw." I was worried that Hunter—or someone protecting his secrets—might arrive at the shop, remember the paperwork that allowed me to transfer data from his laptop, spot the FBI tech, and put two and two together.

"It's the best we can do," he said. "We have you covered if someone comes in. Just give us a call." I hung up the phone and just stood there, processing the exchange.

Why had the FBI asked me again if someone had come in to collect the laptop? Who was the FBI really trying to help, me or Hunter Biden? Why had the agent in Albuquerque refused to take possession of my father's copy of the drive? Why hadn't the agents wanted to see any of the evidence of criminal activity I'd tried to give them in my home?

And now they didn't want to take the equipment, only copy it. Not to mention, it had taken me two days to eventually pull the data from Hunter's liquid-damaged

MacBook Pro. How would they do it in just a few hours? Maybe they only wanted to verify the data and look for child porn. I understood about the porn. It's a federal mandate to prosecute child porn and probably one of the few things they couldn't cover up or sweep under the table. The agents clearly had no intention of copying the drive; I figured they just wanted to make sure it was intact and the property of the original owner—and maybe reunite that owner with his property.

I worried that the phone number I'd been given in case of trouble wouldn't actually protect me. I fully expected Hunter, or a thug representing him, to walk into the shop at any time. I hadn't told the FBI everything, but I'd told them enough. If they went back to the Bidens with what I knew, how long would it take for them to decide how to clean up their mess?

I didn't share my thoughts or suspicions with my father. He had become so disenfranchised with the system, and I didn't want to add to his suffering. I also no longer trusted speaking on the phone. The FBI's lack of caring about what was on the laptop probably meant they were more interested in what the person in possession of it had to say. I had to assume my phone was tapped—and maybe my emails and texts were being read too.

I had plenty of reason to be paranoid.

The agents were going to be at my shop in five days. Something was going to happen, and all I could do—again—was wait.

DECEMBER 4, 2019

A reprieve from my paranoia came on December 4, when the House Senate Judiciary Committee hearings for the impeachment began. My thoughts shifted from potential personal danger to how I could prevent the impeachment if the FBI refused to act on the evidence, let alone take it into custody.

If the Department of Justice and the FBI were running interference for the Biden campaign, I couldn't imagine they would be fair during the impeachment hearings. I would have to get the evidence to Congress somehow. You might be wondering by now why I didn't just go to the press, like some kind of modern-day Deep Throat. Well, I wanted nothing to do with the press. I knew they would just focus on the sex and drugs. They would ignore the damage to our national security and national pride at the hands of the Biden family. If anything from the computer got leaked to the press, the left would call it a smear campaign meant to influence voters. It would quickly be brushed away as a political hit job and nothing more.

Besides, I still believed in the chain of command and felt there had to be established channels to go through to get the information to the proper authorities.

DECEMBER 5, 2019

Nancy Pelosi announced on this day that the House Judiciary Committee would draw up articles of impeachment against President Trump. Now I had only four days to come up with a Plan B should the FBI fail to do their job.

Time was running out.

DECEMBER 9, 2019

Agent DeMeo called around 9:30 a.m. It caught me a little off guard. The only other time we had communicated was shortly after our meeting almost three weeks earlier. He had asked me then to text him the timeline of my interaction with Hunter. I figured that he wanted something in writing showing the chain of custody—or it was an effort to trap me into writing something that could be twisted into a charge of lying to the FBI.

This time, he asked me to text him the model and serial number of the external drive and laptop. I explained that I hadn't made it to the shop yet.

"I need this information before we head over," he insisted. "It's important."

"Give me thirty-five minutes," I responded, then hung up. I finished getting ready and headed to the shop. After texting the numbers to Agent DeMeo, I waited in the shop with the blinds closed and the lights out, so as not to announce that the store was open. Both agents arrived at my door about a half hour late.

"Where's the tech?" I asked, holding the door open.

"We have a change of plans," Agent Wilson responded. "Can we go in the back?"

I led the agents to the back, and Agent Wilson placed his bag on the workbench.

"I have a subpoena here to collect the laptop, the drive, and all paperwork associated with the equipment," he said, pulling out a collection of very formal and important-looking paperwork. "I'll need you to sign it."

I grabbed a magnifying glass off the bench. The document read, "United States District Court of the District of Delaware. Subpoena to testify before a grand jury."

"Hold on," I said. "Testify? Grand jury? This is not what we had discussed. I thought you were just coming in to clone the laptop. I never wanted to testify in front of anyone!"

I read further: "You are commanded to appear in the United States District Court."

"Calm down," Agent Wilson said. "Read towards the center of the page."

I read, "In lieu of personal appearance, see Attachment A." At the top of the last page in bold letters was Attachment A, which listed the laptop and the hard drive with their respective serial numbers.

"You guys scared the shit out of me!" I exclaimed. "So why the change of plans? Don't get me wrong; I'm grateful that you're taking this stuff out of my shop."

Agent Wilson looked over at Agent DeMeo, who was buried in his clipboard. "Ah, Mike?" he said.

Agent DeMeo paused his writing and said, "We have a lab that takes these things and is better equipped than our field tech."

That made perfect sense, and I quickly asked what they needed from me.

"Go over the subpoena. Make sure all the information is complete, and Agent DeMeo will have a receipt for you to sign," answered Agent Wilson.

Agent DeMeo was now on his cell phone requesting a case ID from someone. Agent Wilson asked me to retrieve the laptop, drive, and related paperwork. I went into the locked storage closet and located the equipment. It had been sitting there since April and had the dust to prove it.

Agent Wilson placed the items in his bag, then turned to me and asked, "Is this everything? All the paperwork?"

"Yes, that's everything."

Agent DeMeo ended his call and quickly added the case ID number on the handwritten receipt. "Sign and print here," he instructed, handing me the receipt. It said at the top, "United States Department of Justice Federal Bureau of Investigation receipt for property." The rest had been hastily filled in with a pen.

At this point I was too excited to give anything too much thought. I was just happy this laptop was finally leaving the shop and was in the hands of the authorities. I signed the receipt, and Agent Wilson handed me a copy. Then I stuck out my hand and said, "Gentlemen, thank you for taking your time with this matter, and thank you for getting it out of my shop."

The agents glanced at each other in surprise. I doubt they normally received this kind of a reaction from someone just being issued a subpoena. Agent Wilson eventually shook my hand, saying, "Let us know if anyone comes looking for it. Call us immediately."

"What should I tell them?" I asked, hoping the conversation would never arise.

"Tell them you keep abandoned equipment offsite, like a warehouse location," Agent DeMeo answered, taking over. "Tell them it will take a day for you to check and they should call back the next day. Then immediately text me at my cell number. From now on, only communicate through my cell number. Not Agent Wilson, just me. We need to avoid communicating through, ah, normal channels. I'm sure you can understand. Text me and we will get the equipment back to you and deal with the situation."

Now I felt like I had given away my only good cards and been left with garbage. But it was too late to reconsider; it was done.

"Hey, lads, I'll remember to change your names when I write the book," I joked, trying to defuse the awkward situation with humor.

Agent Wilson kept walking, but Agent DeMeo paused and turned to face me. "It is our experience that nothing ever happens to people that don't talk about these things," he said, before turning back and walking out the door.

I locked the door behind them and sat down at the workbench trying to digest the interaction. Was I being paranoid, or had what the agent just told me been a direct threat, or at best a thinly veiled one?

"But I'm still here," I thought. "The laptop and drive are gone, and I have a subpoena that explains their absence." I believed I was going to be OK, the shop was going to be OK, and my place in the community was going to be OK. I could only hope that the material on the drive would be accessed in time to provide the president with the evidence needed to stop the impeachment sham.

I didn't want to be at the shop anymore. After the morning's events, it felt less like a shop and more like a crime scene.

So I went home and called my father. I was relaying the facts when an incoming call notification showed up: Agent DeMeo.

"I'll have to call you back. I have one of the agents calling in," I told my father before switching calls.

"Hello, this is John Paul," I said.

"Hi, my name is Matt," said a voice I didn't recognize. "I work with Agent DeMeo and Agent Wilson. Do you have a second? I have some questions about accessing the laptop."

Confused, I responded, "Sure, what's going on?"

"Did the laptop come with any cables or a charger? How can I connect the drive to a PC? When I plug it in, it wants to format the drive," Matt said.

"PCs can't natively read Mac-formatted disks. You will only be able to access the drive from another Mac." This is fairly common knowledge among most computer users, and I was surprised that any kind of tech person wouldn't know it.

"Sadly, Hunter never left the charger or any other cables," I went on. "I have a charger and everything you need back at the shop. You guys are welcome to it."

I was feeling really uncomfortable. This Matt guy definitely didn't seem to have the training or resources to be performing a forensic evaluation of the laptop. Hadn't the whole reason for taking the laptop been to get it to a lab for proper evaluation and dissemination?

"Tell him we're OK and we won't need to go back to his shop," Agent DeMeo said in the background.

"We'll call you back if we need to," Matt said before hanging up.

I called my father back and brought him mostly up to speed, excluding this last exchange. When we hung up, I thought, "Maybe this is it. Maybe it's finally over. And maybe there's enough time to get the evidence to the White House's defense team for the impeachment. I've done all I could; there's nothing more I can do."

Then the phone rang.

"Hi, it's Matt again. So, we have a power supply and a USB-C cable, but when we boot up, I can't get the mouse or keyboard to work."

I couldn't believe it—they were trying to boot the machine!

"The keyboard and trackpad were disconnected due to liquid damage. If you have a USB-C–to–USB-A adaptor, you should be able to use any USB keyboard or mouse," I said. He related this to Agent DeMeo and quickly hung up.

Matt called yet again about an hour later.

"So this thing won't stay on when it's unplugged. Does the battery work?"

I explained that he needed to plug in the laptop and that once it turned on, the battery would start charging. I could sense his stress and his embarrassment at having to call repeatedly for help.

"You guys are welcome back to the shop," I reiterated. "I have no one coming in today; the shop would be empty."

Agent DeMeo's response came through as clear as day: "Absolutely not. We're done; hang up."

I sat back and pondered the multitude of possible reasons these FBI agents had chosen to give the laptop to someone who clearly knew very little about computers. Maybe they just needed to be sure of what they had before running it up the flagpole.

I hoped that someone besides me was trying to do the right thing.

THE REST OF DECEMBER 2019

A few days later, on December 12, the Judiciary Committee approved two articles of impeachment against President Trump. He was being charged with abuse of power, acting both directly and through his agents within and outside the United States government to solicit the government of Ukraine to publicly announce investigations into the former vice president, as well as Ukrainian interference in the 2016 U.S. presidential election.

He also was being charged with obstruction of Congress, which felt more like guilt through projection. It was Congress that had been a thorn in the side of the executive branch, demanding countless hearings and investigations centered around proving that Russia, not the American people, had elected Donald Trump. Regardless, the impeachment was going to trial. I just hoped, to spare the nation any additional embarrassment, that the president had the evidence he needed to defend himself.

★ ⚑ ★

Soon the holiday season was in full swing. The shop was busy, brimming with customers full of unrealistic expectations. It didn't take long for me to be distracted and more interested in surviving the season than surviving a politically motivated assassination.

The subpoena was hidden behind a ceiling tile above the workbench. If someone were to come to claim the laptop, I could pull it down as proof that the FBI had come in and taken it.

And apparently, I wasn't the only one thinking about someone coming and collecting the laptop. About a week before Christmas, Agent DeMeo called.

"Hi, John, just checking in. Did Hunter come in asking for it yet?" he asked.

"Nope, no one has come asking about it. Why?" I felt like he knew something but wasn't telling me. He seemed genuinely surprised, and that worried me.

"Well, you know how to get a hold of me if you need us to bring it back," he said. "Merry Christmas."

The red flags sprang back up. I realized that not only was the FBI essentially holding on to the laptop and waiting for its original owner to return, but they had no intention of admitting it as evidence in the approaching impeachment trial. And if that was the case, then I was certain that the FBI had no intention of providing me with protection.

I was back to square one, but this time a whole lot more people knew about the situation and my involvement. And worse, the proof to exonerate the president was now in the hands of a corrupt Justice Department. I knew that the content of Hunter's laptop contained evidence justifying both the phone call to Zelenskyy and the pressure to investigate the former administration...but would the American people ever know of it?

JANUARY 2020

The impeachment trial began. For five days I, along with the nation, watched the president get accused of and attacked for crimes he hadn't committed. On January 22, the prosecutors made their opening arguments. The shit show lasted three days until it was the defense's turn. For the next three days, I kept my fingers crossed waiting for a lawyer to hold up a silver thirteen-inch MacBook Pro and demand a mistrial—the way a condemned man might get a reprieve while sitting in the electric chair.

I waited and waited, but nothing happened. The defense rested on January 28, and there had been no mention of the laptop or its incriminating evidence. This wasn't fair. Hunter's name and some of his questionable activities had been brought up in the three days of questions, answers, and debates, but nothing of what I'd seen on the laptop had been even touched upon. I was convinced that the device was once again locked away in a dusty Wilmington storage closet, or worse, sitting at the bottom of the Delaware River.

Once again, I thought of Plan B: going straight to Congress. I knew I couldn't do it myself, and I was still hoping to keep my business and avoid retaliation from the FBI. Even though it had been a month since I'd spoken with the FBI, I was pretty sure they were still listening in on me. And if they were, I needed to find a way to communicate with my father so he could reach out to members of Congress for me.

I had set up a virtual private network (VPN) for my parents long before, so I could remotely control their devices and troubleshoot any issues they had. I texted my father, and with a little back and forth got him connected to it. Once we had a secure and encrypted connection, I took control of his screen and initiated a FaceTime call.

I then proceeded to fill him in on every red flag I'd encountered, every thinly veiled threat issued, culminating with the laptop's lack of participation in the impeachment trial. I explained my plan, and he suggested approaching my uncle Ron—a retired Air Force colonel, like my father. They also shared a similar background and experience that made them far more appropriate for the task at hand than I was.

My father had already briefed my uncle on the overall situation, not going into detail. He had been more of a safety backup for my father in case my father's involvement with the FBI had gone south. Now it was time to get my uncle up to speed and arm them both with the material they would need to start knocking on the doors of Capitol Hill.

I passed to my father, in a secure file, all the packets of information I'd collected, to be hand-delivered to my uncle. My father would be traveling from New Mexico to Wyoming for a reunion and would be going right past my uncle's house in Colorado. I no longer felt it was safe for my father to have a copy of the drive. The FBI in Albuquerque knew he was in possession of it, and I didn't want to take a chance that the information would spread even further.

My father handed over the copy of the drive and the flash drive with the other documents to my uncle. Everything for Plan B seemed in motion.

Then came a worldwide pandemic, along with Sandy.

FEBRUARY AND MARCH 2020

It was close to closing when a woman walked in clutching a fifteen-inch MacBook Pro. It had a chip issue, and the repair would take about five days, but she needed it for a conference before then. While I have made it a rule not to flirt, hit on, or in any way be inappropriate with female customers, she was the most beautiful woman I'd ever seen. So I wanted to go the extra mile to help her out.

"Let me check it in, and you can borrow one of our loaner Macs and use that for your conference. I can put your hard drive into the loaner, and you'll never know the difference," I told her.

The shop didn't have any loaner machines. I'd be giving her my personal Mac.

When the loaner was ready, her smile lit up the store. I felt like a hero.

★ ⚐ ★

About a week later, she returned from her conference with the loaner machine, and I returned her drive to her repaired Mac.

"Let me know how I can be of assistance to you in the future," I told her, while thinking, "Please let me take you to dinner."

As she walked out, a feeling of sadness welled up. I'd probably never see her again.

★ ⚐ ★

Fate decided otherwise. We ran into each other at my local watering hole, a little tequila bar called Añejo. She sent me a beer as thanks for the repair work, and things took off from there. She sent me a friend request on Facebook, and her profile said she was a photographer, writer, and pilot. She seemed like everything I could ever imagine in a woman: creative, kind, passionate, determined to change the world—not to mention physically stunning.

What her profile didn't say, what she told me later: She had worked for both the FBI and the Department of Defense.

★ ⚐ ★

On March 11, the first case of COVID-19 was recorded in Delaware.

Sandy was deeply concerned about COVID. And Pennsylvania, where she was staying, had initiated a lockdown. I was determined to use this forced isolation to get to know her. We texted daily. I wanted to know everything about her.

She'd been born in Germany, but her family had moved to Delaware when she was a baby. He father had been in the military, but her parents had divorced. Sandy then found herself in a single-parent home with a mother who seemed to want little to do with her. And she told me over text that her efforts to make her strict military father proud had finally culminated in her joining the FBI and later the Department of Defense.

I reread that just to be sure: "I joined the FBI…"

You can probably guess where my mind went from there. I was at the center of a potential FBI investigation. Who was Sandy really? Was she an FBI honey trap? She seemed introverted, highly intelligent, and creative. It would be so easy to build the profile of my perfect woman from my social media content.

"If it looks too good to be true…" kept going around in my head. But what if it was just good enough to be true? What if I'd finally met "the one"? Abandoning this developing relationship now could mean missing out on the chance of a lifetime.

Returning to my senses, I texted back: "What did you do for at the FBI?"

"I was an asset analyst. But I got out shortly after 9/11."

"What about 9/11 caused you to leave the agency?"

"I was there."

She had been working at an FBI building a block away from the World Trade Center. She had shown up for work early that morning, and it was shaping up to be a beautiful day. She decided to go to the parking garage and grab her camera out of her car. As she was walking back across the street, the first plane flew overhead.

She instinctively pulled her camera from her bag, just in time to photograph the fireball erupting as the plane collided with the first tower.

The event gave her PTSD. I would later discover that she anonymously donated all the photographs she had taken to the National September 11 Memorial & Museum.

I asked her about her DOD work. She said she couldn't talk about it, but what she'd seen or found out about there had been bad enough for her to leave the DOD, cast away her conservative views, and become a liberal. She was now working as a photographer.

I sighed. Not another one. But at least now my FBI honey trap theory was dissolving, because an FBI agent with access to all of my data would never set me up with a liberal.

In any case, on March 20, Delaware went into full COVID-19 lockdown—no traffic between states. She was trapped in Pennsylvania, and I was stuck in Delaware.

May 2020

Lockdowns finally eased, and on May 24, Sandy and I went to a drive-in movie and restaurant. I felt like a sailor who'd been lost at sea spotting land on the horizon. I couldn't take my eyes off of her. For the next few days, I was on cloud nine—my mind much more focused on her kisses and not at all on any potential FBI honey trap. And certainly not on Plan B for Hunter Biden's laptop.

But of course the plan had already been put into motion. My father and I FaceTimed on the secure VPN so he could update me. Things were not going well, to put it mildly. He had called the offices of U.S. senator Lindsey

Graham (Republican of South Carolina) and Congressman Jim Jordan (Republican of Ohio). Both calls had been met with rejection.

He had sought legal advice and been instructed to speak only with a lawyer, so he'd been requesting to speak with the politicians' lawyers. But no one would pass along the request without knowing what it was about, and my father couldn't share that with just anyone.

My uncle Ron wasn't faring any better. He didn't have my same qualms about the press, and had reached out to investigative journalist Sharyl Attkisson. No response. He had reached out to White House correspondent Bret Baier. No response. He had sent a message directly to the White House notifying them that he was in possession of data important to national security. You know where this is going: no response.

He had just sent information by email and snail mail to the activist group Judicial Watch but had not heard back yet. He also was planning to reach out to U.S. senator Ron Johnson (Republican of Wisconsin) that week if no one else responded.

No one wanted to touch this with a ten-foot pole, it seemed.

My father and uncle had been out there knocking on doors with information that was highly important for national security, but no one would open the door. Was it because of the global hysteria over COVID-19? Was it because of the previous three years of Russian conspiracy witch hunts? Or was everyone afraid of being caught in a disinformation tsunami and having their credibility or career ruined?

Maybe it was my fault. Maybe I had failed to provide my father and uncle with the right tools and the right verbiage for them to be taken seriously. Maybe I needed to step out from the shadows and take ownership of the situation.

But if I did this and the liberal Sandy found out, she would murder me in my sleep.

And I was falling in love with her.

★ ⚑ ★

It took only about a week of spending time with Sandy in person for politics to put a wedge between us. She had been working on a COVID disinformation research team, and now began bombarding me with negative texts.

"How can you support that animal!" she wrote, referring to President Trump. "I don't understand you. I wish I could talk with your exes and see what it is that attracts you to liberal women."

I tried to defend myself, but she wouldn't let me get a word in.

"I can't picture myself with someone that shares the same views as a conservative," she wrote.

I pleaded with her to not do this, that my actions should speak to my character and not to judge me like this. Something must have triggered her, but I didn't know what.

"Don't text me again," she finally wrote. "We'll talk about this tomorrow."

I was heartbroken. I'd already been feeling abandoned by the FBI and our leaders in Congress. Now I was feeling it in my heart.

We talked briefly that night, but it seemed hopeless. When I said goodbye, I fully expected it to be the last time I'd get to hear her voice. I felt broken and defeated. I had managed to screw up my romantic life while the rest of my life fluttered directionless in the wind. It seemed as if for over a year now, I had been personally responsible for all the bad situations I found myself in.

June 2020

Tension was high in Trolley Square. A number of protests over the murder of George Floyd had led to the vandalization of several businesses downtown. Another weekend of protests was rumored, culminating with a march scheduled for June 5. Business owners were nailing plywood across their windows and doors.

Feeling depressed by my recent breakup yet reluctant to succumb to fear, I planned to sit outside my shop and stand guard. If someone approached the shop with bad intentions, I would hand them a bottle of water—hoping the kind gesture would spare my business from damage. Better for someone to hurl a plastic bottle than a brick at my shop. I collected cases of water in preparation for the coming weekend.

By Friday afternoon, Trolley Square was a ghost town. Businesses were closing early, and the whole place was boarded up. I was ready, armed with water bottles and good intentions. It had been quiet all morning, but that had more to do with the relaxed COVID-19 rules and people heading off to the beach for the weekend.

I was about to step out for lunch when Sandy walked back into my life.

She had brought a bag with some of my belongings to return, and we ended up talking. We sat on the porch for hours. My angst over the pending riots dissolved in the heavy rain of an unexpected evening thunderstorm. When the sky cleared, we ended up in my hammock, spending the whole night there covered by the shadows of the leaves in the moonlight. I had never felt such a close connection with anyone in my entire life.

I hadn't lost her. I'd been given a second chance at happiness.

I wasn't going to waste it.

★ ♫ ★

I began a stealthy art project using plywood from the boarded-up stores, now no longer needed, that the owners gave me. I designed a one-foot wooden heart with the word "One" suspended in the middle. From the bottom point of the heart ran a two-foot spike for driving the heart into the ground. I wanted to have at least forty done and planted around Trolley Square by the following Friday, one week after the rained-out riots. I thought that if I could turn material that had been used out of fear into a symbol of togetherness and love, it would make our community stronger.

On Thursday night, I dragged out all of the wooden hearts and placed them in stacks on my porch. The bars let out at 1 a.m., so I waited patiently until the streets were quiet. The Trolley Square shops have front and back parking lots, with strips of manicured landscaping between the sidewalks and the parking lots. This is where I planned to plant my hearts.

The mission took about an hour and went off without a hitch. I went to bed that night with a sense of great accomplishment, not just for the act of recycling fear into hope, but because my skills at creating things with wood were improving and maybe could lead to something a lot more than just tinkering in the basement.

I decide to build a studio for Sandy, for her creative pursuits, on the third floor of my home. It was going to be expensive—she had very good, and pricey, tastes. Over the next few weeks, I looted my shop of all my excess vintage Mac equipment to fund the project.

And I asked my mother for one of my grandmother's rings to give to Sandy—not to propose, but just so she'd have it. My mother found a ruby ring that her father had given to her mother during the war. It was perfect.

Sandy loved it, and I loved how happy she was—and how happy she made me.

But this apparent fairy tale did not have a happy ending.

August 2020

I was working on Sandy's studio in the summer warmth when she unexpectedly stopped by the house.

"I have amazing news!" she yelled up the stairs.

I came down the stairs and walked into my bedroom, where she was sitting on the bed with her laptop.

"What is it?" I asked.

"You know how I've been a part of the COVID-19 disinformation team for the past few months?" she said. "I've been invited to join another team."

"What's the subject?"

"A panel to block and debunk the Joe Biden, Hunter, Burisma, and Ukraine theory," she stated proudly.

I froze.

What the hell? My suspicions of her being a honey trap swooped back en masse. Why, out of the blue, out of all the people on earth, was my girlfriend joining a team that wanted to debunk the truth about the Biden family and their Ukrainian grift? Was this a way to get me to expose what I knew or reveal my intentions?

Maybe the Feds were poking me with a stick to illicit a reaction or get me to disclose my plans.

"What's wrong? I thought you would be happy," she said, as I sat there motionless, contemplating this turn of events.

"I'm sorry. Of course I'm happy for you!" I quickly answered. "That sounds exciting. I'm so very proud of you!" But worry chewed at my insides.

Even if she weren't working with the Feds, she might very well discover in her research that I'd had a laptop belonging to Hunter Biden and been trying to get someone to notice the Bidens' dirty laundry. Which would for sure be the end of our relationship.

I had avoided political conversations as much as possible and had kept my secret from her completely. Now I became afraid that my reluctance to talk about it would raise her suspicions and have her question my politics.

Turns out I was right.

★　🏳　★

We were both sitting on the porch enjoying a glass of wine one evening when she turned to me and asked, "Did you fill out your mail-in ballot?"

"I don't think I'm going to vote this year," I responded, hoping that would put an end to the conversation.

"You have to vote!" she insisted. "It's important that you show your support for Biden."

"I don't want to vote for Biden," I said. "I'd rather not vote at all."

"But if we weren't dating, you would vote for Trump!" she yelled.

"You don't want me to vote for Trump, but you want to force me to vote for someone I don't like?" I asked, puzzled and defensive.

"Why don't you like Biden?" she asked.

"It's personal."

"I knew it! You're all the same. You're just another right-wing QAnon asshole, sucked in by Fox News lies! Why don't you go and shoot guns with your conservative buddies?" she shouted.

I had no idea what she was talking about. I didn't even know what QAnon was, nor did I have any conservative shooting buddies. She was attacking me for no reason, and I couldn't get her to stop. I couldn't tell her the truth about what I knew about the Bidens; she would never have believed me.

She stormed out of my house.

We emailed a bit in the days after, and finally I gave her a choice. We could try to work together and get through this, even if that included couple's therapy, or she could give me the ring back.

A few days later, my grandmother's ring showed up in the pile of mail at the foot of my door.

It was over. I felt a deep sadness and loss, but at the same time I knew the hurt would be so much greater if I had allowed the relationship to continue. I also knew I would never find a woman like her again. She was about as perfect for me as I could ever imagine, aside from her inability to get past politics.

I will always love her.

August 22, 2020

The day the ring was returned, my friends Kim and Allen called. They could tell I was upset, so they invited me over to their place for a scotch. Allen is a lawyer, and back in the summer of 2019 I had asked him generally about the legality of being in possession of something that someone abandons.

The two-mile walk to their house helped clear my head. And my friends and Allen's twenty-two-year-old bottle of scotch gave me comfort. Out of that comfort came confidence. I now had a gut feeling of what I had to do. I'd been freed from a relationship that had prevented me from stepping out from the shadows and taking responsibility for getting my story and the truth out.

"So, if I had seen something on a computer that was criminal and affected national security, and I feared for my safety, besides the FBI and Congress, who should I contact?" I asked Allen.

Just as the words came out of my mouth, I realized I already knew the answer. Before Allen could respond, I answered my own question: "The president."

"What have you gotten yourself into?" Allen asked.

It felt liberating to explain what I had been through over the previous year and a half. I didn't go into details, but I provided the basic framework. And then we discussed how to reach out to the president directly.

Then it dawned on me that I had a solution already laid out nearly a year ago.

"Rudy Giuliani!" I exclaimed. "He was my safety net should something happen to me."

Allen agreed that going to the lawyer of the president was the smart thing to do and offered the most legal protection. I felt good, like this was the direction I needed to take. And finally, I felt like I had the courage to take it, to see things through.

August 26, 2020

I spent a few days trying to track down a way to contact Rudy Giuliani directly, to no avail. The contact request page on the website of Giuliani Security & Safety, his company, would have to do. I took my time composing the message, wanting to give enough information to show the big picture and with enough details to make it impossible to ignore. And it all had to fit in the website contact field.

Here's what I wrote.

> For almost a year I have been trying to get the contents of Hunter Biden's laptop to the proper authorities. I first reached out to the FBI and they came and collected it, but I have reason to believe they have destroyed it or buried it in a filing cabinet. After months of waiting for something to come of this, I can only assume that members of the FBI, who are against the President, have it and it will never be seen again. Luckily, for my protection, I made several copies and I have been trying quietly to bring it to peoples' attention. I am reaching out

to you for assistance and making sure the people that need to know about this, do.

I have email proof that the Quid Pro Quo started on May 12, 2014, with a request from Vadym Pozharskyi to have Hunter and Devon use their influence at the White House to pressure the Ukraine Government to stop investigating Burisma. This was one month after Hunter was appointed to the board. I have emails from Blue Star discussing White House conference calls and meetings about Ukrainian policy and discussing Vice-President Biden's trip to Ukraine being sent to Vadym Pozharskyi directly. I have proof that the Office of the Vice-President was selling Influence and support to foreign nationals in exchange for money. The selling started with the US's support of Ukraine which helped them land the IMF load in early 2014. Reward for that support was provided in the form of board posts for Hunter and Devon and an initial large sum for each of them in the range of $1,295,000 and a monthly check of $33,000 each. This allowed for direct access to the White House and included favors from visas to putting pressure on a foreign government by a private citizen. I feel the closer we get to the election, the more this will be ignored. Please help me get this information to people who can use it and bring justice to people that deserve it.

I hit submit and stared at the "Your message has been sent" alert that popped up. There was no going back now; the message was out there and my name was on it.

Rudy Giuliani was a controversial character. He was vilified on the left and championed on the right. Most important for me, he was a lawyer and had spent the summer of 2019 researching the very content I'd been sitting on. I was worried that handing this information to him would guarantee the perception that the motive was a political attack.

But I had sent the request. And now, yet again, all I could do was wait.

August 27, 2020

Robert Costello, a lawyer representing Rudy Giuliani, responded to my website request by email, saying he would be very interested in speaking with me. I replied with my phone number and told him I would be free after 7 p.m.

Finally, a response! Maybe not from Rudy, but at least I was talking with a lawyer.

I left work early, and a few minutes past 7 p.m. he called.

"This is Bob Costello. Is this John Paul? I understand you have Hunter Biden's laptop. Can you email me a couple of files from it?"

"Sure. I only have a copy of the laptop; the laptop was subpoenaed last December by the FBI." I immediately emailed him a couple of documents, then said, "Check your inbox."

"OK, I got them," he said. He started to read out loud what I'd sent, and I began to suspect that someone else was secretly on the line with us—maybe Rudy Giuliani himself, listening to see if what I was offering was bullshit or the real deal.

"What do you want from us?" Bob asked.

"I want this to get in the hands of the appropriate people. If there can be any legal or physical protection for me, that would be great too."

"And you say the FBI has had the original since December 2019?" Bob asked.

"I can send you over the subpoena."

"They wanted you to testify before a grand jury?"

"No," I answered. "It said in lieu of an appearance, they were to take possession of the laptop, drive, and paperwork."

"Let me tell you about the Department of Justice," Bob said. "When Rudy and I returned from Ukraine last year, we submitted over two hundred subpoena requests to the district attorney, and not a single one has been filed. Do you know what the term 'slow walking' means?" I said no.

"It's when they deliberately drag their asses to delay or even prevent a case from moving forward," he supplied. "That's what the DOJ is doing to us, and that is what the FBI is doing to you. How quickly can you get me a copy of the drive?"

"I can drop something in the mail for you tomorrow."

"Let me call you back in a few minutes," Bob said. "Will you be around?" I said yes, and we hung up.

That wasn't so bad! I had their attention, and it felt like I was talking to the right person. At this point I realized I needed a copy of the drive. My copy had all my notes, and because of this I felt it would be considered tampered with. My uncle Ron had the copy that originally had been in my father's possession. That was too far away.

Then I smiled, remembering that the other copy I'd made back then had ended up with Kristen, and she was to hand-deliver it to Rudy Giuliani if all else failed. It was kind of funny that I could have saved myself nearly a year if I had just gone to him in the first place.

Bob called me back, and we agreed I would FedEx the drive to him the next day.

"You're an honest guy, John Paul. Are you sure we can't do anything for you?"

"Does Mr. Giuliani drink scotch?"

Laughing, Bob responded, "Sure does! Macallan, I think. I'll ask."

"I don't want Rudy to know who I am. I'm still trying to run a business and live in a community in the lion's den. That said, once this whole ordeal is over, if Rudy wants to pick out his favorite bottle of scotch, I wouldn't kick it out of bed."

Bob started laughing again. "I like you. You're a good guy. Your secret is safe with me, and I'll see about the scotch…"

When we hung up, I dialed Kristen.

She answered quickly. "Is everything OK?" she asked. "What's wrong?"

"Everything is OK," I said, then amended that: "I think everything is going to be OK. I hope it's not too late. I need to come over and grab something."

AUGUST 28, 2020

I dropped the drive off at FedEx the next morning on my walk to work. It was done. The drive was on its way to the lawyer of the president. My work was done; I'd seen it through to the end.

That evening I FaceTimed my father with the news. He asked me what kind of protection Rudy's people were providing. I realized I had yet to ask for any. But I didn't feel scared anymore. Biden was mostly hiding in his basement, seemingly uninterested in doing whatever it would take to win the presidency.

In contrast, President Trump was holding rallies attended by tens of thousands.

I had nothing to fear from the Bidens. I had the president's lawyer on my side, and the president was a popular and powerful man.

AUGUST 29, 2020

Bob called saying they had received the drive. I gave him instructions on how to safely access it and avoid connecting it to the internet. He was speechless for a few minutes as he verified the contents.

"This guy is a real piece of work," Bob said as he waded through the ocean of porn on Hunter's desktop.

"I warned you," I said, laughing. "That guy is gross!"

I walked him through the emails and pointed out the some of the more interesting files.

"He has forty-eight thousand emails in this one folder!" Bob exclaimed. "We're never going to be able to go through all of this. It will take months. There's a good chance that you know more about what happened in Ukraine than anyone else alive. How many months did you spend going through this?"

"About three," I answered.

Bob asked if I had seen anything about China. I told him I'd seen one or two things, but that wasn't what I'd been interested in.

"I'm going to have my team focus on China," he said. "Can we rely on you to help fill us in on Ukraine? You know where everything is. You've had months to examine the material, and you can get to it a lot quicker than we can. Time is running out, and we could use your help."

I agreed, and over the following week I assisted Bob in accessing the data relative to the Burisma grift, funneling along emails and documents I'd discovered over a year earlier. I gave him what I'd tried to give the FBI and later Congress. This time someone was paying attention and taking it seriously. I was filled with pride now for my actions, not fear. I felt that the truth now had its best chance of getting out there.

The following week, I assisted Bob in making bootable copies of the drive so other people he was working with could have access. I didn't need to know who these people were, and my identity was kept a secret as well. I didn't want to be known. This was not what I wanted to be famous or infamous for. I still had a life to live, and I didn't want this to even be a chapter in my life story.

Plus, if I wanted to keep my business and my status in the community—which I very much did—I didn't want to be blamed for Joe Biden's losing the presidential race.

★　🏴　★

After I passed on to Bob and his team what I knew about Ukraine, things started to quiet down. I began planning a trip to Colorado. It was a good time to catch up with my aunt and uncle there, and with my parents coming up from New Mexico, it would be the perfect time to have an in-person briefing. Knowing my father would query me on the status of my protection, I did ask Bob about providing some level of security in case something went south. He told me he had two retired NYC detectives located outside Philadelphia, and they could be at my home in thirty minutes. That would likely be enough to get my father to relax.

Although it felt like everything was coming together, I was still uneasy. We were now less than a month and a half away from the election and nothing about the laptop was in the news.

Yet.

SEPTEMBER 23, 2020

Senator Ron Johnson and the U.S. Senate Committee on Homeland Security & Governmental Affairs released a report on Hunter Biden, Burisma, and corruption. This was what I had been waiting for. The drive and its data must have found its way to Senator Johnson's desk, and his team had acted on it.

Reading through the report, I saw a good deal of information there, but much was missing.

I read about how the former Russian mayor's widow had given Hunter $3.5 million, and about the millions Hunter brought in from China and Ukraine while his father was vice president. I saw a wealth of dollar signs but no explanation as to how Hunter and Devon had earned any of the money or what services they had provided. There was no sign of the laptop and its data in the report at all.

The laptop had never made it to Senator Johnson's desk.

I felt panicked but also excited. I could get in touch with Senator Johnson's office and provide the missing pieces for his report.

SEPTEMBER 24, 2020

I went to Senator Johnson's website and was relieved when I saw a whistleblower link under the contact information. I clicked it and quickly filled out the form, pasting in a letter I'd written the night before.

Good day Sir,

On April 12th 2019, Hunter Biden came into my shop and requested data recovery for his MacBook Pro. After performing the service, he never returned to the shop to collect his Mac or his back up. After the 90 day abandonment time period expired, I started to go through his drive to see what was on it. Once I realized what was on his computer, who was involved, and the effort people may go to prevent me from talking about it, I reached out to the FBI. After meeting with the FBI, they came to my shop on December 9th and presented me with a subpoena for his Mac and the backup. A few months later, the whole Quid Pro Quo impeachment circus started and I knew that the FBI didn't do anything with Hunter's Mac or we would have seen evidence of it during the impeachment trial. The fact that Blue Star was funneling sensitive information out of the White House and sending it to Vadym Pozharskyi was never mentioned. The initial request, back in May 12, 2014 , one month after Hunter joined the board, for Hunter to use his influence to pressure the Ukrainian government to stop putting pressure on Burisma and its owner was the initial Quid Pro Quo and was never brought up. This leads me to believe that the FBI either destroyed or locked away Hunter's Mac and back up. Fearing this, I had made a backup before reaching out to the

FBI. I live and work in Wilmington, Delaware and my life and business would be destroyed if word got out of what I have done, so I have been very careful to hide my tracks and keep a low profile. Apparently, it's a lot harder to be a whistleblower when you're on the Right than the Left. After reading your report, I feel safe to reach out you and provide you with what I can. I have included copies of some emails as well as the subpoena from the FBI. I hope you can find this information helpful moving forward. All I ask is that my business and person remain anonymous. Thank you for your hard work in seeking justice.

Cheers

I hit submit and waited. I checked my email multiple times that day, waiting for a response to arrive. If the senator's office were to reach out when I was in Colorado, it would be five or six days before I could furnish them with any info from the drive. On top of that, when I returned, there would be only a month left before the election.

The clock was ticking.

THE REST OF SEPTEMBER 2020

Still no word from the senator's office as I boarded the plane for Colorado. But when the plane landed, there it was: a new message from whistleblower@ronjohnson_senate.gov. It read:

Hello,

To assist us please provide the following information:

1. Are you a U.S. citizen?
2. What is your full legal name?
3. Why did FBI/DOJ request these materials?
4. Why did you not provide them voluntarily?
5. Have you had any further contact with the FBI or DOJ?
6. Are you represented by counsel?
7. Provide the contact information of the FBI agent(s).

Thank you.

The email was strange. The formatting was off, and it looked like someone had hastily copied and pasted the questions into it. There was no formal introduction or digital signature at the bottom. It looked like a teenager had written it, not someone in the office of a senator. And those questions…nothing was being asked about the Senate report or the laptop. They focused only on me and my involvement with the FBI.

I started to get a bad feeling about having reached out to the senator. This was not the response I'd been expecting.

Then I got a voicemail from a number with a 202 area code—Washington D.C.: "Colonel Mac Isaac, this is John Solomon, the investigative reporter. You may have seen me on Fox. I would love to talk to you about Hunter Biden.

I think you and I know some joint things together. If you have a chance, please give me a call."

I knew who John Solomon was. While I was doing my research back in 2019, he also had been engaged in the hunt to get to the truth about what the Bidens had been up to in Ukraine. The problem I had was that he made his living as an investigative journalist. The media, both good and bad, make a living selling sensational stories. All of Hunter's drug use, his fondness for prostitutes—as evidenced by text messages found on the laptop—and other illicit behavior, would overshadow the true crimes of influence-peddling and risks to national security.

Sex sells. That's how journalists and media organizations make their money. The last thing I wanted was to align myself with a career journalist.

So, why was the journalist John Solomon calling my cell phone, asking to speak with my father? As far as I knew, only the FBI and my immediate family knew about my father's involvement. I hadn't even mentioned my father to Bob Costello in Rudy Giuliani's office.

I was puzzled and, moreover, concerned. How had my number been leaked to the press?

★   🏳   ★

My father picked me up from the airport in Colorado, and I shared the new developments on the hour-and-a-half drive. He thought the email I'd received, supposedly from Senator Ron Johnson's office, might actually have come from someone at another agency. In case it was the National Security Agency or Department of Justice, he advised me to respond truthfully—because this is how agents could burn you or catch you in a lie. He also demanded that I find out how John Solomon had gotten my number and suggested that I reach out to Bob when I got to the house.

Once we arrived at my aunt and uncle's house, after a round of hugs and greetings, I pulled out my Mac and replied to the email.

1. I am a U.S. citizen
2. John Paul Mac Isaac
3. I approached the FBI after I realized the potential danger I was in due to the sensitive nature of the contact. I wanted to get rid of the Mac and the drive and I thought that going to the FBI was the best option.
4. I wanted them to have it and gave the Mac and the drive to them, voluntarily.
5. I was contacted a day after they collected the Mac and drive. They did not have the tech support necessary to take a look at what was on the Mac, so I helped them over the phone. I was told by them that if Hunter or anyone else came in asking for the equipment back, I was to contact Mike DeMeo immediately and they would return the Mac and drive the next day. A couple weeks later, Mike DeMeo contacted me to see if anyone had come

in asking about the equipment. I said 'no' and that was the last I heard from them.

6. I am not represented by counsel. From the beginning I have wanted nothing to do with this, but to pass it along and hopefully, prevent anything from coming back on me or my business.

7. Special Agent Joshua J. Wilson (only agent on the paperwork)

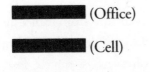 (Office)

█████████ (Cell)

Special Agent Mike DeMeo (the agent I was to contact in text only if someone came looking for the hardware)

████████████████████████

Let me know if you require any additional information.

Then I called Bob and explained the situation. He said he would make some phone calls, adding: "I know John Solomon personally and will tell him that you and your father are off limits." He said he would call me back in an hour. A little feeling of guilt twisted inside me, as I hadn't told Bob about sending the whistleblower email.

Not satisfied, my father called John Solomon directly.

"This is Colonel Mac. You called looking for me earlier?" my father barked into the phone. "How did you get the number you dialed?"

He listened, then told me: "He said he got your contact information from a mutual friend in D.C."

John wanted to sit down and have a longer conversation, but my father wasn't having it. "When I'm ready to talk, I'll let you know," he said, then disconnected the call.

A few hours later Bob called back.

"So, John says he was given your info from someone at Senator Ron Johnson's office. Did you file a whistleblower report yesterday?" he asked. Shit, news travels fast. I told him yes.

"Well, I told John to leave you and your father alone, so you shouldn't hear from him again," Bob affirmed. I thanked him for his help and hung up.

What the hell! My contact info had been leaked to press less than twenty-four hours after I'd filed a whistleblower report! I'd thought whistleblowers got to remain anonymous. I'd just watched an impeachment trial with a case revolving around a whistleblower whose identity was kept a secret. And my identity had been leaked by the very people I was trying to help. Now I was pissed off.

By the next day, I had cooled off a little, but I was still agitated and wanted a response. I fired off an email to the whistleblower account for Senator Ron Johnson's office.

Good afternoon. I am reaching out today to follow-up from last Friday's request for information. Moving forward can you please provide me with someone to be a point of contact. I would prefer that Whistleblower not be listed in my inbox, I hope you can understand. While you're at it, is it possible to get an email address or contact information for Attorney General Barr so I can avoid filling out the DOJ's default contact form. Thank you in advance for your time and effort.

Cheers!

Call it cheeky or call it passive-aggressive; I just wanted to move forward.

In any case, I had a briefing to perform. My uncle Ron, my father, and I descended into the basement. I told them both the entire account for the first time, from the evening Hunter had walked into my life until the email I'd just sent. My father had heard many of the details, but my uncle hadn't.

We all agreed that something else needed to happen. The U.S. presidential election was thirty-eight days away, and the American people still didn't know the truth. I still hadn't heard back from Senator Johnson's office, and it was quiet on the Rudy Giuliani front.

"Maybe we should go to Tucker Carlson," my uncle suggested. "My friend's neighbor knows a former Fox news executive named Ken LaCorte. I have his contact information; I can reach out."

As much as I wanted to avoid the press, things were getting down to the wire. We all agreed to have my uncle reach out and share with Ken some of the files and the basic timeline of events. Still feeling a little guilty over not telling Bob I had approached Senator Johnson, I called him now and told him our plan to reach out to Tucker.

"You think you can get this to Tucker?" Bob asked.

"We're going to try, as long as you don't think it will interfere with what you're working on."

Bob didn't see a conflict. "Watch the debate on Tuesday," he added. "The president is going to bring up Hunter, China, and Ukraine."

"No shit! The president has seen it?" I was astounded that finally, *finally*, the laptop's contents had reached the person who needed to see it most—and that he would act on it.

"Rudy is briefing him on it right now," Bob said. "Don't worry, you're still only known as 'Bob's guy.'" Relieved, I thanked him for the update, and we hung up.

The first televised debate between President Donald Trump and presidential contender Joe Biden was three days away.

★ ⚑ ★

In the morning, I said goodbye to my family and hopped in the car with my father to head back to the airport. Once again, he lectured me to keep my head on a swivel and my wits about me. He was uneasy. He knew a lot could happen in the coming month, and we would be too far away from each other for him to be of any immediate help if needed.

★ ⚑ ★

I returned to work and tried to go about my day as if everything were normal. But I couldn't wait for the debate, couldn't wait to hear what President Trump would do with the information I had supplied him with through Bob.

I couldn't wait for the American people to finally hear the truth.

With the genie out of the bottle, my safety would be guaranteed. There would no longer be a secret I could get killed over. I just prayed that the source of the information and my identity would remain a secret.

That afternoon, I received a response to my cheeky second message to Senator Johnson's office. It said that someone from the office would contact me next Monday at noon.

There was nothing to do but help customers and wait.

That evening my good friend Chip and I convened around the TV to watch the first presidential debate. We watched closely, waiting for a mention of any of the Biden family's secrets that the president now knew about.

And then it was over.

No mention of pay for play, Ukraine, or Burisma. Just two old guys snapping at each other for an hour and a half. What the hell? All the American people saw that night was a tired old man and a rude, loud one. It was embarrassing.

More important for me, the truth hadn't gotten out.

I was still in danger.

October 5, 2020

The phone rang around noon on Monday.

"Hello, John? This is Kevin from Senator Johnson's office. How are you?"

"Fine. How can I help you?" I had been awaiting the call and had a collection of documents pertinent to the Senate report at the ready.

"I have two gentlemen here on the line from the NSA. They would like to ask you some questions."

"Sure," I answered cautiously.

They interrogated me for an hour. They asked if I belonged to a government agency, foreign or domestic. They asked if I had ever worked for a foreign power or on behalf of one. They asked about any political organizations or other groups I might be affiliated with. They asked if I was a paid informant for the FBI or DOJ.

Then the interrogation traveled to the topic of Russia. Had I ever been to Russia? Did I know any Russians? Had I communicated with, posted on, or contributed to any Russian media or social media outlets?

I had started answering all of these questions with a touch of humor, but after thirty minutes of being grilled and not being asked a single question about the laptop, I grew frustrated.

Finally, after they questioned my honesty, I'd had enough.

"When are you guys going to ask me about Hunter, Burisma, and Ukraine?" I asked.

"That's not what this call is for," one agent replied.

"We have enough," the other agent added. "We'll let you know if we have any further questions."

They ended the call, and I sat down. I had been pacing for the previous fifteen minutes. This was bullshit. Why was I being questioned while the true criminals were walking free? Why was I being made to feel so guilty by the people I was trying to help, for doing the right thing?

Going to Senator Ron Johnson's office clearly had been the wrong thing to do. It had exposed me to the media and put me on the radar of another government agency. Thanks, Ron.

October 6-10, 2020

The rest of the week crawled. I hadn't heard a peep out of my uncle or Bob. I didn't want to bother them, but I hated getting this far and still not knowing what was going on. Luckily, Bob called on Friday.

"So, we worked out a deal with the *New York Post*," he said. "They're going to run three stories covering Burisma, China, and some personal stuff. I just wanted to give you a heads-up. Someone might reach out to you from the *Post*. She's OK, but don't talk to anyone else."

"Am I completely out of the story? I can't be quoted! No one can know that I'm the source!" I frantically responded.

"Calm down. They agreed to keep you out of the story; they just need to verify you exist, and it's not an interview," Bob reassured me. "You'll be OK. There's nothing to worry about."

My heart was pounding. It seemed as if every time I took a phone call, the circle of people that knew about me grew exponentially. Now not only was the press involved, but they wanted to talk to me. And I certainly didn't want to talk to them.

I decided to hide out at home, so no one could find me at the shop. No one but the FBI knew my home address—not even Bob, since I'd used the shop as the return address for the FedEx package. (And I'd never had a chance to give him my address for sending the scotch.) Then I'd go in on Sunday, when no one would be expecting me at the shop, to do repairs.

If the press wanted to talk to me, they'd have to find me first.

October 11, 2020

I went to the shop Sunday morning as planned. It was a cold and dreary fall afternoon, and Trolley Square was deserted. I'd told my friend Allen, the lawyer, that he could swing by and I'd upgrade his 2009 iMac, and he showed up with a six-pack of Amstel Light and his computer. Allen had been continuing to give me legal advice, and I thought upgrading his iMac was an easy way for me to show my appreciation.

We sat inside with the blinds drawn. Only the lights over the bar were on. To the outside world we were closed, and the shop looked vacant.

We were on our second beer when a knock sounded on the door.

We both looked at each other. I placed my beer on the counter and walked over to the door. The temperature difference between inside and outside had caused the inner door to fog up, and I couldn't make out who was knocking.

I opened the door to a woman wearing a COVID-prevention mask and clutching an iPhone.

"Can I help you?" I asked, expecting her to show me a broken screen or a failing battery.

"Are you John Paul?" she asked.

My knees went a little weak. "Yes," I said.

"My name is Gabrielle Fonrouge. I'm a reporter for the *New York Post*. Do you have a minute?"

I stepped forward so the inner door could shut behind me. I didn't want her to see Allen or think there was anyone in the shop listening.

"What can I help you with?"

"Did Hunter Biden come into your shop and leave a laptop?" she asked.

My brain started spinning. Should I call Bob and make sure this was the reporter I was supposed to talk to? All the newspaper names sounded interchangeable, and I couldn't remember in the moment which ones were liberal and which ones were conservative.

"It's OK," she said, seeing my apprehension. "Bob sent me. I'm just here to verify who you are. It's standard procedure before a story gets published. He said you were handed a subpoena by the FBI. Can I see it?"

I told her to give me a minute. As I walked into the back to retrieve the documents from the ceiling, Allen made frantic hand gestures encouraging me not to reveal his presence.

I returned with the paperwork, and Gabrielle inspected it.

"Can I get a copy of these?" she asked, handing the papers back. I didn't see the harm, and I already had images of the documents on my phone, so I texted them to the number she provided.

"What about the paperwork signed by Hunter?" she continued.

"The FBI took the original, but I took a photo of it before they did. Hold on," I answered, scrolling through a year's worth of images on my phone.

"Can you show me any files? Bob said there was home-made porn. Can you show me that?"

"I don't feel comfortable sharing that type of personal information with you." If she was working with Bob, then she already had access to the drive. She didn't need to get it directly from me.

"Is there anything you can show me?" she asked.

"Bob has everything. I'm sure he would be happy to show you," I said, then repeated: "I'm sorry, I just don't feel comfortable."

We chatted for a minute, then she thanked me for my time and said goodbye. As she made her way to her car with no one in sight, I called out: "I can't have my information leaked. It would ruin my business!"

"Don't worry, we keep our confidential sources confidential. Oh, and tell your friend peeking through the blinds he can come out now."

I laughed. "Hey, how the hell did you guess to look for me here on a Sunday?" I asked as she opened the car door.

"I'm a good reporter," she answered.

I liked her. She'd been easy to talk to, and I felt like I could trust her, but I was still worried. Should I have given her those copies? I wished someone had coached me on what to say—and what to keep quiet about.

I went back inside and locked the door behind me.

"There's no stopping it now," Allen pointed out. "Once it's out there, it will no longer pose a threat to you. The word will be out, and people will hear about it. There's no way to keep it quiet anymore."

"Great," I responded sarcastically. "As long as nothing points back to me!"

OCTOBER 12, 2020

Gabrielle texted asking that I contact her immediately if anyone from any other media outlets reached out to me. A fresh wave of angst hit. Why, all of a sudden, would other outlets know? Why was she concerned about the possibility if my identity was being kept secret? There was a lot to think about, but I also was planning to stay focused on work in case the next day was busy, as Tuesdays had so often been.

However, all the planning in the world could not have prepared me for what I would go through two days later, when the story came out, and what I would endure in the weeks that followed.

PART THREE

THE FALLOUT

October 14, 2020

The night before the story went up, I don't think I ever fully slept. I hit refresh on the *New York Post*'s website about every five to ten minutes. Then, very early in the morning on Wednesday, October 14, the home page changed to display an image of Hunter and Joe Biden.

The headline was: "Smoking-gun email reveals how Hunter Biden introduced Ukrainian businessman to VP dad."[2]

There it was, in living color: the truth. I scanned the article, looking for any mention of my name or where the emails had originated. "The computer was dropped off at a repair shop in Biden's home state of Delaware…"

That seemed to hit a little too close to home, but I thought it was a good article and kept reading. I had been hoping to see more exposure of the influence-peddling and other white-collar criminal activity, and less of the sex and drugs, but I understood the game. And at this point, I finally felt like I was safe. The truth was out there. It wasn't my secret anymore. I had nothing to fear.

And then the emails and notifications started flying. By 7 a.m., people were responding to Facebook posts I'd been tagged in.

"I hope you rot in prison" was posted under a review Sandy had made me write for some bamboo sheets. Below a post with a photo of my aunt Kathy and me leaving church was the comment, "Does your Aunt Kathy know what a horrible piece of shit you are?"

I'd never really done much on Facebook besides thank people for birthday wishes and promote my business. I barely knew how to post, let alone delete and block other users. After a quick Google search for how-tos, I started frantically deleting comments and posts, but they were coming in too fast to keep up. At least Sandy had coached me on keeping my page private.

That's when I noticed that a lot of the people posting were my so-called friends. The full effect of the situation slowly sank in.

Community members and friends were turning on me.

I felt eerily calm, perhaps like a man on death row who has come to terms with his fate. I was no longer afraid of being killed for my secrets, but after spending an hour deleting hate-filled posts, I now strongly feared retaliation again—only this time from a mob instead of a single family. How had so many people figured out right away and with such certainty that I was the owner of the unnamed repair shop in Delaware?

At about 8:30 a.m., a caller solved the mystery.

"You don't know me, and I'm not here to attack you," said the caller, "but you need to contact the *Post*. They forgot to blur out your business's name at the bottom of the signed work authorization. They need to remove it now!"

I immediately hung up and called Gabrielle.

"We have a big problem!" I snapped. She said she would take care of it personally and that she was so very sorry. About thirty minutes later, she texted to let me know that it had been a mistake by the art department and it had been resolved.

"I'll make sure whoever was responsible gets fired," she added. "Hopefully, we got to it in time. Again, I'm so sorry that this has happened."

But it was too late. Calls had already begun bombarding the shop—mostly from members of the press at first, then from angry people. I deleted my Facebook page to put a stop to that avenue of hate, but the calls kept coming.

Many of the haters had a common theme: that I would do prison time.

"I hope you get raped in prison."

"I hope they throw the book at you."

"I hope you get what's coming to you when they throw you in jail."

What were they thinking I'd done? None of my actions in the previous year and a half had seemed illegal. Getting arrested had never even been a blip on my radar. Yet now, besides the occasional email and phone call telling me to go f—k myself, everything seemed centered around the idea that I'd broken the law.

Soon the comments also began linking me to Russia.

"Eat shit and *die* Russian stooge."

"Putin thanks you for your service."

I was confused. Then Chip called.

"Hey, buddy, are you OK?" he asked. "Dude, you broke the internet."

"What are you talking about?"

"Twitter and Facebook are blocking the story. It's all over the news. They're protecting the Bidens by preventing the story from getting out."

I was dumbfounded. I knew that Twitter and Facebook were biased and left-leaning. They had spent the previous four years blocking and silencing conservatives on their platforms while promoting the leftist agenda. This was nothing new; I just figured it was how all big California tech companies operated.

But to openly run interference for a Democratic presidential candidate—that took something more than balls. Twitter was blocking the entire *New York Post* from posting on its platform. Facebook was restricting any conversations related to the story. The left-leaning tech platforms had become willing tools of influence wielded by their Democratic masters. How could the truth get out when it was being blocked by social media, and more than 86 percent of Americans receive news from digital devices?[3]

I'd heard of things going viral, but this was the digital version of the polar opposite. But how were these companies justifying their actions? I searched Google for an example of what I might see if I tried to tweet something about the story, given that I wasn't on Twitter myself.

"This content is restricted due to presence of hacked material" read the message that someone had posted from a direct message Twitter had sent. Twitter was even blocking the discussion from its private messaging system. I was stunned at the political overreach, but at least I now knew why people were labeling me a criminal.

Twitter was blatantly implying that I was a hacker.

But I was no criminal—in fact, all I had been trying to do all along was *expose criminal activity*! I felt like the best way to show that was to just go about my business. I refused to hide. I wanted to be accessible to those who questioned my integrity. I wanted to be able to look my accusers in the eye and defend my actions. I needed to stand up for myself, because it now felt like half the country was against me, with no defenders in sight.

After a night of restless sleep at a friend's house, I took an Uber home at around 10 a.m. so I could take a much-needed shower and get ready for work. My street was quiet and void of cars. I cautiously unlocked my door and walked in. Besides the greetings of hungry cats, the house was quiet and empty. I had placed my phone on vibrate to silence the inundation.

I got ready and then slowly walked to the shop, trying to clear my head and prepare myself for what might lie ahead. So far, as violent and threatening as things had been, I had yet to experience any physical harm. But now I was picturing an angry mob congregating in front of my shop, waiting for the focus of their anger to arrive.

A group of people were indeed waiting outside my shop, most holding Macs. I sighed in relief as I walked up to the door. Then the questions started flying, and I realized that perhaps only half of the people waiting were actual customers.

"If you are not here for service, please respect the people who are," I said to the crowd, then opened the door. Puzzled customers proceeded to follow me in.

"What's going on? Are they from the press?" asked one customer. I allowed him in and motioned for the others to step back outside. Then I locked the door.

"It's a long story. What brings you in?" I answered, realizing that given social media's Herculean efforts to suppress the story, there was a good chance these customers weren't aware of it.

I locked the door between customers, just as I'd done at the height of COVID, letting in only one person at a time and asking if they required service before doing so. By midafternoon, six reporters were camped out in front of the shop, all eager to get in.

The day was busy, and I was surprised by how little people knew of the situation. Many of the customers I had already seen would not still have been customers if they'd known.

"Maybe it'll be OK," I thought. "Maybe my business won't be affected."

Then I forgot to lock the door behind the last customer of the day.

The gang of six reporters pushed past both me and the customer.

"I think I caught you at a bad time," the customer said. "Maybe I should come back later."

"Please don't go," I pleaded. He left.

For over an hour, the reporters tore me to pieces. They had pinned me back behind the bar and were blocking the exit route to the door. Even though everyone had masks on, they pushed in much closer than the recommended six feet of social distancing. I felt cornered and threatened.

One after another, they hurled questions and accusations at me. I had already expressed my lack of interest in discussing the story, but they persisted. They explained that the more I remained silent, the more that people would assume I'd done what I'd done for political reasons. They told me I should trust them, and they promised to paint what I told them in a favorable light. Then they started to question my integrity.

I started to crack.

I wanted to defend myself but also didn't want to comment on my family's involvement. And I didn't want to embarrass the members of Congress who had ignored my family's effort to get them the material. In the end, after I repeated "I don't feel comfortable talking about this" and "No comment" at least a hundred times, the frustrated reporters' tone shifted from wheedling to downright bullying.

"We're not going to go until you tell us what happened," one reporter stated. "We're going to keep coming back until you tell us what we want to hear."

I knew if I stayed in the shop, it would only get worse.

"I'm sorry," I said. "I have to go to lunch, and I need to ask you all to leave." I'd finally found the resolve to get out, and I pushed my way through the pack of wolves, adding: "It's time for everyone to go."

I locked the door behind me, praying they didn't notice my hand shaking. Then I walked down the length of shops and headed up Gilpin Avenue, never once looking over my shoulder. I just needed to get home.

When the door was safely shut on the outside world, I sat on my living room couch and called Bob.

"How are you holding up?" he asked.

"I just spent an hour and a half with the press. They wouldn't leave me alone."

"The best thing you can say right now is 'no comment.' Anything you say, they will try to twist, distort, and use to catch you in a lie," Bob said. "It'll get easier from here on out. The story's out, and the news is spreading. They'll leave you alone in a couple days."

I didn't know if I could tolerate these kinds of attacks for even a couple more days. I thanked Bob for the coaching and spent the rest of my lunch break lying down and figuring out my next course of action.

The shop door would stay locked, period. I would make some signs for the door requesting that the press respect my customers and their privacy by not entering the shop. I would write another note to my customers apologizing for the uncontrollable circumstances that had led to the locked door, and requesting that appointments be made for future service requests.

Feeling better with a plan in place, I headed back to the shop, practicing saying "no comment" on the walk over. As

I approached from across the parking lot, I saw that only a few people were waiting. It became apparent that they were all customers, thankfully.

I wasted no time posting the signs on the door, then entered the shop and turned the lock. Surprisingly, all my customers seemed oblivious to the morning's events. While hateful missives had been destroying my online world, no one had caused trouble in person. In fact, strangers occasionally would knock on the window and wave or give me a thumbs-up. A few people even greeted me at the door by saying thanks.

This positivity gave me the confidence to go about the rest of the afternoon as if nothing had happened, although I did change my traditional "How can I help you?" greeting to "Do you have a technical question?" This would help keep anyone from the press, if they were to show up, from getting past the door.

When it started to get dark, I pulled the blinds—no point giving anyone outside an illuminated target. After an hour with no customers, I decided to close up early and go home. I was about to kill the lights and head out when my phone rang.

"Hey! How are you holding up?" my friend Kristen asked.

"I'm hanging in there. It's been a long day, and I'm heading home."

"Well, don't leave just yet. There's a cute blonde reporter shooting live out in front of your shop!" Kristen exclaimed, laughing.

I killed the lights and leaned flat against the wall.

"I can still see you on TV," she said, laughing a bit again.

I darted into the back room. I was so mentally exhausted, all I could think about was going home, locking the door, and killing the lights.

"Don't worry, she works for Fox," Kristen said. "And it looks like she's done. Text me when you get home."

I thanked Kristen and waited until the spotlight beamed at my shop was extinguished. Once the crew had packed their bags, I made my exit. As I was locking the door, a voice behind me said, "Tough day?"

It was the reporter. Kristen was right; she was really cute. I just smiled, still reluctant to talk to any reporter regardless of which side they were on—or how cute they were.

"In your interview today, why did it seem like you were protecting someone?" she asked.

Wait, what? I hadn't done any interviews.

Maybe she was referencing something I'd told the media wolves that morning?

"I would do anything to protect the people I care about," I said. I was totally in the dark, but it was true in any case.

Then I turned and went home.

★ 〽 ★

Bob called around 8 p.m.

"I listened to your interview today," he said. "Sounds like they came at you pretty hard."

The mysterious interview again.

"What interview?" I asked.

"Someone from The Daily Beast recorded you when you were answering questions," Bob answered. "You didn't know they were recording?"

"I had no idea."

"How bad was it?" Bob asked.

"Wasn't great!"

Bob chuckled. "It wasn't horrible either," he said. He gave me a few more pointers and reiterated the need to repeat "no comment." Then he asked about security: "Anyone give you a hard time?"

I told him that so far, there hadn't been any physical hostility, but that I did feel a little uneasy—as if things were a little *too* quiet.

"Do you still have the number for those two detectives in Pennsylvania?" I asked. Better safe than sorry.

"Let me check on getting someone out to you if you need security. Call me if something happens."

After the call, I was beat and decided to try to sleep, even though it wasn't even 9 p.m. yet. But I was completely alone, and I heard every floorboard creak from my prowling cats that night. Every conversation of bar patrons pouring into their cars after last call prodded me awake.

Every sound seemed suspicious now.

October 15, 2020

I woke up feeling pretty good, all things considered. I weeded out work emails from hate mail, and found the occasional message of support, which made up for the negativity tenfold. Then I checked the voicemails sent to the shop.

"I'm going to meet you at the shop at 11. Bring your mother so I can…" I shut off the message. It wasn't even the nastiest I'd heard so far. But the number was from area code 856—right across the river in New Jersey. This was a disgusting and noticeably upset person, only fifteen miles and a two-dollar toll away. It was unnerving.

The shop was mostly quiet when I arrived. Someone had placed a crude handmade sign in front, showing their support. Another person had added a less flattering message at the bottom of it, accompanied by bags of dog shit. But my own signs on the doors were working, and I had to avoid the press only when I left and returned from lunch.

But then the calls started again and never seemed to stop. Maybe one in ten was an actual customer. Most calls were quick bursts of anger or death threats, with the caller quickly hanging up. Some callers asked how I could live with myself.

Eventually, I just stopped answering the phone. I even removed the batteries from the store phones.

That evening, while I was with a customer, two guys knocked on the window and were looking in. They were wearing hoodies pulled over their heads, along with face masks.

"We need you to look at our Mac," the tall one stated when I opened the door. "Can we grab it? It's in the car."

I said sure and returned to the bar with my customer. But both men were still standing there inside the door.

"I thought you had a problem with your Mac?" I said loudly.

The two men looked at each other, turned, and walked out.

"What was that about?" my customer asked.

"I don't think they were here with a Mac problem," I said, going to the door and locking it. From now on, I'd leave the blinds down. And look more closely at anyone knocking before I opened the door.

★ ⚑ ★

I avoided every dark doorway and dim streetlight on my way home. Luckily, it was an active Thursday evening, and I felt safety in the numbers of people on the streets. Chip and a rather large fruit basket with a thank-you card were waiting on the porch.

"What's this?" I asked, ascending the porch steps.

"No idea," Chip said. "It was here when I got here."

We both stared silently at the large, colorful basket.

"There is no way in hell I'm eating anything from that basket," Chip finally said.

I knelt down to inspect it. "I don't know. Some of it looks pretty tasty," I said, feeling a little hungry. "Maybe the stuff in tins isn't poisoned."

I suggested we get it off the porch and into the house so as not to draw attention.

"No way!" yelled Chip. Then, more softly: "What if the FBI has it bugged, and they're hoping you bring it in the house?"

I instantly stood up and backed away from the basket. We quietly pondered the true purpose of this gift some more, until I picked it up and unceremoniously dumped it into the trash can alongside of the house.

"Good idea," Chip said.

We hung out for most of the evening. We ordered takeout, and I tried to relax. I was glad he was there. I didn't want to be stuck at the house alone, like the previous night. We watched TV and settled in for a quiet night.

Then, at 10:46 p.m., a text from a number I didn't recognize popped up.

"JP, I'm Larry Johnson. I'm on the phone with your dad. Old friends. Trying to do a three way call," it read.

My father had only two best friends that I knew of, and Larry Johnson wasn't one of them.

"OK," I tentatively responded. Soon the call came through.

"Hi JP, this is Larry Johnson. I think I have your father on the call as well. Colonel Mac, are you there?"

"I need you to shut up and listen to what this guy has to say," my father instructed. "He has experience in these situations, and you need to do what he says."

"I will," I replied.

"He has killed people. Have you killed people?" my father bellowed. "You will do more than 'I will.'"

"Yes, sir."

Larry introduced himself and then asked how I was holding up. I briefly described the previous two days.

"It is very important we get you security and protection," Larry said. "Your life is in danger, and we need to make sure you're safe." He told me to call Bob Costello immediately after we hung up and demand that someone come to my house as protection "now!"

He went on to warn me not to trust anyone. People would find a way to record me, to catch me saying or doing something that could be twisted and used to attack me. If I was out in public, I was not to talk about anything related to the situation. I was never to be alone at the shop, or on my way to and from it.

"Above all, get Bob to provide you with the security he promised. He owes you that," Larry concluded.

At about 12:30 a.m., I texted Bob: "I know it's late, but I've been advised to get some security personal down to me soon. Nothing is imminent, but things are getting heated. Also, I think it's time I get a lawyer. If you can assist, that would be fantastic. Again, sorry to bother you this late. Cheers!"

So much for a quiet and relaxing night and an early bedtime.

OCTOBER 16, 2020

The phone jolted me out of a rock-like sleep at 8:30 a.m.—it was Bob. He asked why all of a sudden I needed a lawyer and security.

Keeping things vague and Larry's name out of it, I told him I'd been instructed to ask for assistance.

"Any chance you could be my lawyer?" I half-jokingly asked. "Or at least recommend someone?"

"There's no way I can represent you," he said, "but I'll make some calls. Give me a couple hours, and I'll have someone get in touch with you about security."

After we hung up, I texted Larry a summary of the conversation. He called for a status check a few hours later. I told him I hadn't heard back yet and would text him as soon as I did.

About five minutes later, Larry texted: "It is very important that we get you a lawyer."

"But I haven't broken the law."

"The main reason you need a lawyer right now is to send cease-and-desist letters to everyone who's claiming that you're a Russian agent. They need to retract and apologize or face legal consequences of defamation."

It made sense. But right now it was 10:35 a.m. and I had only twenty-five minutes to finish getting ready for work.

★ 🏴 ★

Some new decorations awaited me outside the shop: a large patriotic poster thanking me for my service, and half a dozen smashed eggs.

"Hey friend, how are you doing?" came a voice behind me as I surveyed the scene. I turned and saw Amado, my friend from the local bar scene and an avid Mac fan who frequented the shop, usually bringing a pack of Amstel Lights. Amado is a very large Black ex-Army man from Sierra Leone, West Africa. I was glad he was there; no one in their right mind would try to mess with me while this mountain of a man was on watch.

He sat out in front of the shop as I cleaned up the egg detritus. Shortly thereafter, Bob called, informing me that a gentleman named Beau Wagner would be getting in contact with me.

"He's a crusty old New York City detective, but he's a good guy," Bob said. "I would trust him with my life. He'll be able to take care of your security concerns."

I told Bob of my newly acquired bodyguard, and he laughed. Then I texted Larry, briefing him on the developments, and went about my day.

Larry texted back later that day with the names of two lawyers: Brian Della Rocca and Jacob Flesher. I still hadn't heard back from Bob, so I was inclined to trust Larry's judgment. If my father trusted him, I trusted him.

He texted again that evening, telling me to download an encrypted instant-messaging app called Signal and then contact him on it. When I did, he informed me that I was now under investigation by the FBI and that moving forward, we should use Signal to protect our conversations.

"Why am I under investigation? I've done nothing wrong!" I asked, panic rising in my chest.

"You're at the center of a new investigation centered around the possibility that the laptop is part of a Russian disinformation scheme," he answered.

"Here we go, using the 'Russia excuse' again," I thought. Out loud I said, "But the FBI has sat on this thing for almost a year. How can they get away with calling it Russian disinformation now?"

"It's what sells newspapers and gets people's attention away from them and on to you," Larry explained. "All that matters is you have to be careful. Your phone and communications are being tapped. So are your parents'. You need to get them on board with Signal and watch what you say. They're going to try to catch you in a lie or trick you into an obstruction charge. Now more than ever, you have to be careful who you talk to."

It turns out that earlier that evening, Adam Schiff (Democrat of California), an outspoken House member who'd led the charge in the president's false impeachment, had gone on CNN and told the American people that the laptop story was part of a disinformation campaign put in place by the Kremlin to interfere with the 2020 election. Either his statements had gotten the attention of the FBI or he'd requested that they investigate. Either way, I was now at the center of a completely different FBI investigation—as its target.

"Do you know how to make a forensic image of the hard drive?" Larry texted. "If so, make one and I'll get it to my cyber intelligence guy, Yaacov Apelbaum. If not, Yaacov can come to you."

I didn't think I could make a forensic image—the files were only dragged and dropped—so Yaacov would contact me in a few days. Not long after, my phone rang with a New York City area code.

"Is this John Paul?" asked the rough-sounding New Yorker on the other end. "This is Beau. Bob said you needed some help."

At last, some security help! He said he knew a Wilmington detective and would reach out to him to get some form of police involvement. He also said I needed to reach out to the Wilmington PD and file a domestic terror threat, to help protect me from any crazy person who chose to act on a death threats.

Beau said if anything were to happen, I was to call him immediately.

I spent the rest of the night in the house, listening to the babble and bustle coming from the bars down the street. And I slept a little better that night, knowing that help and security were coming.

OCTOBER 17, 2020

A Wilmington patrol car greeted my arrival at the shop the next day. An officer got out and approached me.

"Good morning. I'm here to keep an eye on things," he said. "Either I or another police officer will be parked here as long as you're open."

"You have no idea how happy you just made my mother!" I exclaimed as I shook his hand. Of course, I was very grateful too. It was a relief to have someone watching out for me. I personally thanked each arriving officer; the Wilmington PD's above-and-beyond support was amazing. They even dispersed the members of the press that had congregated, awaiting my return from lunch. To think I had been worried about approaching local law enforcement for fear they would turn me over to the Bidens! Again, I could have saved a year-plus of bullshit. As it would turn out, the police officers were my biggest supporters.

Larry texted at lunchtime, asking me how I was holding up. He said that Brian Della Rocca, one of the two lawyers, was going to reach out to me, and that if all went well, he would be the one defending me.

The phone rang not long after.

"Good afternoon. My name is Brian Della Rocca; I'm a lawyer over here at Compass Law. How are you today?"

"I'm OK. It's a little crazy, but Wilmington PD has been keeping an eye on me, so I feel safe."

He told me that Larry had given him a rundown of what had happened, and asked about whom I had talked to and what I had shared. He said he wanted to start to build a wall around me to protect me from any more potential attacks. I gladly accepted his offer of help, and we started the formalities of his becoming my attorney.

★ ⚐ ★

That evening after work, I met Kristen and our mutual friend Greg at Añejo, the tequila bar. After being only in my house or at work for so long, I was climbing the walls and a margarita sounded great. It didn't hurt that Greg was a large guy no one would want to mess with.

We sat outside, with me facing the sidewalk. It didn't take long before someone I knew approached and started asking questions. They started off innocently enough: "How are you? Are you doing OK?" Then they quickly shifted to "So how much money did you get?" and "Are you really a Russian agent?"

"Does he look like a Russian agent?" Greg interjected, coming to my defense.

"Maybe a Scottish agent," I said, trying to make light of the situation. I was wearing a Scottish military hat that looked like a beret with a pompom on top; a pin of my family's crest adorned one side.

As the margaritas went down, my caution lowered too. Armed with liquid courage, I felt more compelled to challenge attacks on my character. Most of the attacks focused on the idea that I had profited in some way from the whole awful experience. Also that I was a pawn for the people

I'd gotten involved with—whether the Kremlin or Rudy Giuliani—and that I'd been played. The general consensus seemed to be that I was an idiot who'd been conned into doing what I did.

By this time, I couldn't care less what people were saying. Eventually, I grew tired of these conversations and started saying "*dasvidaniya*" to the instigators until they left us alone. I was three sheets to the wind and feeling zero pain.

The pain would come tomorrow.

OCTOBER 18, 2020

The phone's ringing jackhammered into my ear the next morning.

"Hello, is this John Paul?" a foreign-sounding man asked.

My splitting headache and memory of joking about Russia the previous night made me hesitate.

"Speaking," I eventually answered.

"My name is Yaacov." Larry's cyber intelligence guy. "I am about two hours out from Wilmington. I need your address please."

That meant about two hours to clean myself up and try to tame the hangover beast. I swallowed some Tylenol, drank a ton of water, and crawled back into bed for a while.

After jumping in the shower, I waited for him on the porch. It was shaping up to be a beautiful day, and the cool autumn breeze eased my throbbing head.

"John, it's Yaacov." I slowly opened my eyes to see him standing at the bottom of the porch steps.

"Come on up," I said. "If you don't mind, I need to see some identification."

Yaacov reached into his wallet and held out a card. It was a black-and-white ID, similar to a military one. My visual disability and bleary, bloodshot eyes made it hard to read, but it looked like it said "Yaacov Apelbaum." I couldn't make out the rest, but it looked official. I knew Larry had worked at the CIA for twenty-eight years and that was how he knew my father. If Larry sent this guy, it had to be OK. I had to trust him. Larry seemed to know things before they happened and was one step ahead of the FBI.

We sat down at the dining room table, where I had set up a Mac and my working copy of the drive. I sat there quietly as Yaacov pored over the drive's contents. He was the first person to sit down with me and show a real interest in the contents as well as in the knowledge to access them.

He asked about the timeline of events. He asked about how the laptop had come into my possession, and how I'd gotten it to the FBI. His attention turned to the suspected criminal activity. At long last, someone was sitting across from me at the table and listening to what I had to say!

I told him everything, then repeated what I'd told Bob the night before the *Post* story broke: "At this point, I would be OK in losing everything as long as the truth gets out and there is justice."

Bob had reassured me that it wouldn't come to that, and that I'd done the right thing. But now a deep sadness welled up. I had lost my anonymity. Death threats were arriving every hour. Police officers were parked in front of my shop all day, and after last night, I thought I might never go out in public again.

I eventually lost it. As embarrassing as it was, I started to break down and cry in front of Yaacov—a complete stranger. Although I was thrilled that someone was finally taking an interest, it felt like it was too late and the damage had been done. And I couldn't help but feel guilty, as if I had betrayed my customer's privacy through my actions even though the laptop had been my property at that point and contained evidence of criminal actions. Yaacov reassured me that I had done nothing wrong, but my actions had permitted a customer's personal information to go public. Could anyone ever trust me again with their devices?

"If there is criminality here, we will find it. From what I have seen so far, it looks like there is," Yaacov said. "You did the right thing."

I tried to calm down but was embarrassed about crying in front of a complete stranger—it looked weak. And if I'd learned anything over the previous few days, it was that people can sniff out weakness and will use it against you.

Yaacov asked more questions, and I pulled myself together enough to answer. Finally, he closed the Mac's lid and said, "I'm going to take this with me."

"What, the drive?" I asked, puzzled.

"Yes, the drive and the Mac."

"Why?" It was the only copy of the drive in my possession, and the Mac, even though pieced together from parts at the shop, was still worth some money.

"We need to get this to a safe place so we can inspect it. It's the closest thing we have to the original," Yaacov said. "We need to generate actionable intelligence and share it with law enforcement agencies."

On the one hand, he was willing to do what the FBI had failed to do with the original, what I'd wanted them to do all along. On the other, I felt like I needed to maintain access to that drive for my safety. A lot of my personal notes and research findings were on it.

I asked if I could copy some personal stuff off the drive before he took it.

"Sorry, I can't have anyone else access this drive," he said.

I wasn't in the mood to protest, and I understood the need to preserve the chain of custody. So, as with the FBI, I ended up handing over a laptop and drive in the hope that the truth would get out and some good would come from it.

But after Yaacov left, I was too emotionally exhausted to have much hope or feel any good. I felt like my world was crumbling around me, and the hangover sure wasn't helping.

★ 🏳 ★

Brian, my new lawyer, texted later that day: "Did you get my email last night?"

"I'm sorry, my inbox is tough to go through right now, so I've been avoiding it."

He'd sent more paperwork to fill out and sign. Yaacov had also emailed, asking to be placed on a retainer and for me to give Brian his contact info.

Brian and I agreed to meet at 8:30 a.m. the next day, Monday, to go over the details and sign the engagement letter. As reluctant as I was to get up that early, I was eager to get started with legal representation.

OCTOBER 19, 2020

Once I got set up as Brian's client, he was blasted with requests for interviews with me. He published a statement saying that I wasn't giving interviews at this time, but he kept getting interview requests, and I kept getting death threats and hate mail.

More bad news soon followed.

An article went up saying that the FBI was investigating Hunter's laptop as being part of a foreign operation.[4] Earlier that day, Director of National Intelligence John Ratcliffe had gone to the media explaining that the laptop situation was not about Russian interference. Now, the normally secretive FBI was sharing with the world that I was at the center of an investigation into a foreign operation to interfere with the 2020 election.

On top of that, fifty former intelligence officers had all penned a letter saying that the *New York Post* story sounded like Russian disinformation. These were not just a bunch of armchair analysts or mailroom guys; these were former directors from every intelligence agency in our government.

John Brennan and Leon Panetta from the CIA; Russ Travers from the National Counterterrorism Center; Glenn Gerstell, general counsel from the National Security Agency and the Central Security Service; Richard Ledgett, the former deputy NSA director; Marc Polymeropoulos, a retired CIA senior operations officer; and Cynthia Strand, who'd served as the CIA's deputy assistant director for global issues—all signed the letter without ever seeking the truth.

The mainstream media had a field day with it. Pretty much the entire nation now thought I was a hacker working with the Russians.

October 20, 2020

At 11 a.m. I met with a Wilmington police officer to follow up on the hate mail and threats. I showed him what I was dealing with, saying I couldn't care less about a guy crying into his keyboard in San Diego, but the growing number of local haters was disturbing. These were people who could come into the shop or worse, follow me home. The police cruiser out front provided a feeling of safety at the shop, but I still had to get to and from work.

The officer advised me not to go out in public alone, and said he'd get some additional patrols along Delaware Avenue and have them keep an eye on my house. I forwarded all the hate mail I had to him and thanked him his time. He waited until another officer arrived before leaving.

The shop echoed with emptiness when he left. Apparently, someone had posted about the situation on Nextdoor—described as "an app for neighborhoods where you can get local tips, buy and sell items, and more." The "and more" often seems to include neighbors complaining about one thing or another. The news seemed to now be spreading like wildfire. Someone even posted about what business should occupy the location when I was forced to close my shop.

The toughest post to read was titled "The Mac Shop at Trolley Square." It felt like the entire community was out to trash me, believing I was involved with the Russians and should never be trusted again. And I had no way to delete or block these posts, no way to control the lies and misinformation people were spreading.

These were my neighbors and customers. And, I realized with a sinking heart, they were also my friends.

OCTOBER 21, 2020

Four or five smashed tomatoes on the sidewalk made for an ugly red carpet the next morning. One of the large supportive posters had been ripped down and torn in half; it was sticking out of the trash can. At least there was no dog shit, but I'd still have to clean off the sidewalk.

The day was slow. I mostly spent it filtering emails and screening calls. Some customers came in to collect completed repairs, not drop off new ones. Many of them were clearly uncomfortable. They said as little as possible, sliding over their paperwork and a credit card and avoiding eye contact. A few looked at me with distrust, as if I had rifled through their hard drive. Others expressed their disappointment and said it was the last time they would do business with me.

One customer came in just to tell me that he didn't want his Mac back, and that I'd never get a dime out of him. He said if any of his personal information were to get released, he would hold me directly responsible. I tried to reassure him, but he went on a rampage about how I was a fascist pawn who would get what I deserved. The officer in the parking lot came in before it could escalate beyond that.

Everyone has a right to be upset. America is a free country, and people are allowed to nonviolently express themselves. The expression he left me with was, "I hope you lose your business."

Without any new repairs coming in, it was looking like his hope might come true.

★ ⚐ ★

I went home early, partly because the shop was dead and also because I wanted to walk home while it was still light out. I sat down and checked the news. It looked like some clever reporter had researched the case ID included on the receipt the FBI had given me for the drive. It turns out that it was linked to a money laundering case out of Baltimore. Huh?

Agent DeMeo was based in Baltimore, but he'd never said anything about money laundering. The only discussion about anything remotely close to money laundering revolved around Ihor Kolomoyskyi and his Delaware assets. I remember discussing that, but it hadn't involved Hunter Biden.

Why was Hunter's laptop listed on a receipt for an investigation that had nothing to do with Hunter? It must have been a way to hide the device.

The reporter had caught the FBI in a lie. How would they explain their way out of it?

In any case, the next presidential debate was tomorrow. And an unnamed business partner of Hunter's supposedly was coming forth with explosive evidence. There was no way the truth could be hidden from the American people after that. Twitter couldn't suppress the debate, claiming hacked material. Facebook couldn't block the broadcast and restrict its distribution.

Maybe once the truth was out, the community would forgive and forget. Maybe my customers would return.

As with so many times previously, all I could do was wait and see.

OCTOBER 22, 2020

The day of the final presidential debate, the shop was mostly quiet again. Just a few customers picking up their devices. I spent the morning shuffling emails to my attorney and the Wilmington detective investigating the death threats—unfortunately part of my morning routine now.

If something didn't change soon, my business wasn't going to survive.

I eagerly awaited the debate, hoping that President Trump would bombard Joe Biden with every example of dishonesty that Joe had exhibited throughout his campaign. I wanted the president to call out Joe's corruption and greed. Exposed in front of the American people, Joe would be forced to admit to his criminality or get caught lying, trying to cover it up.

This would help exonerate me and hopefully bring customers back. I believe in "If you see something, you should say something," and I shouldn't have to be afraid for my life or my business by taking that responsibility seriously.

And I was hopeful that the surprise revelations would help. Right before the debate, there was to be a press conference with Tony Bobulinski, a retired Navy officer and a former business partner of Hunter's. It seemed he was desperately trying to get out in front of an ongoing FBI investigation.

So I eagerly tuned in to the press conference that evening.

Tony said he had a meeting with the FBI the next day and was prepared to hand over three cell phones, which he claimed contained evidence that Joe Biden had in fact profited directly from his influence as vice president. He spoke mostly of a partnership with businesses linked directly to the Chinese Communist Party.

I knew little about any dealings with China. With Hunter's laptop, my focus had been on the criminal activity in Ukraine. So this was news to me, and I was hoping the rest of the country was watching—and, more important, believing. Apparently, a lot of the emails on the laptop relating to China had also been addressed to Tony. Even though Tony's efforts to go public stemmed from self-preservation, they hopefully would vindicate the laptop, showing it as legitimate and authentic, not some part of a Russian disinformation scheme.

And they might have, if any news station other than Fox had aired the press conference. I didn't need the half of the country that believed me to hear Tony's confession; I needed the other half to hear it. Once again, the mainstream media and social media were coming to Joe's rescue by not giving Tony a platform.

But I still hoped that the story would be exposed during the debates.

★ ⚑ ★

Early on in the debate, Joe's cognitive decline was already starting to show. He said President Trump's ineptitude had caused the virus, before quickly amending "virus" to "lockdown." I actually felt bad for Joe, who'd been hiding in his basement during the last legs of his campaign. Or maybe forced to hide. The way he was paraded around in front of the cameras, then randomly forced into isolation—seemingly without any say or autonomy—made me feel like I was witnessing a case of elder abuse.

The two candidates sparred over how each had been handling COVID-19. It was tough to watch, this political weaponization of a global tragedy.

"Move on," I thought. "Get to the money."

Then it came.

Trump: Joe got three and a half million dollars from Russia. And it came through Putin, because he was very friendly with the former mayor of Moscow and it was the mayor of Moscow's wife. You got three and a half million dollars. Your family got three and a half million dollars and you know someday, you're gonna have to explain—why did you get three and a half? I never got any money from Russia.[5]

I knew that "three and a half million" was a reference to a gift that the former mayor of Moscow's widow had given to Hunter. It was a bullet point in Senator Johnson's report.

But the president's attack quickly turned to how tough he was on Russia and then to this:

Biden: I have not taken a penny from any foreign source ever in my life. We learn that this president paid 50 times the tax in China, has a secret bank account with China, does business in China, and in fact, is talking about me taking money? I have not taken a single penny from any country whatsoever, ever, number one. Number two, this is a president—I have released all of my tax returns. Twenty-two years. Go look at them. Twenty-two years of my tax returns. You have not released a single solitary year of your tax return. What are you hiding?[6]

So the president was forced to abandon his assault to defend himself on the topic of taxes. When the subject of national security as it related to Russia and China did finally arise, Biden was quick to redirect attention away from anything potentially insinuating about his own actions.

Biden: We are in a situation where we have foreign countries trying to interfere in the outcome of our election. His own national security advisor told him that what is happening with his buddy— well, I won't, I shouldn't—I will—his buddy Rudy Giuliani. He's being used as a Russian pawn. He's being fed information that is Russian, that is not true.[7]

This was not helping my case. I needed the president to shoot down Joe's claims with facts, but those facts never came. The American people had been told that the FBI was investigating Russian interference, and Congressman Adam Schiff had called the laptop part of a Russian operation. Now the Democratic presidential candidate was basically saying, though not in those exact words, that the laptop had come from the Kremlin.

Joe Biden is a career politician and very skilled at lying. During the debate, his lies didn't stop with Russia either. He swore that his son had never made a dime off of China. Then, pointing to the president, Biden stated: "The only guy that made money in China is this guy."

I couldn't believe what I was hearing. I had seen the emails. I knew how the Biden family had accumulated a chunk of its wealth. I knew that Joe had used his family members to hide millions in income. His ability to flat-out lie to the American people was impressive—and horrifying.

But why wasn't President Trump calling bullshit? If Rudy had given him the drive, he had the proof. This was the last opportunity to have an unfiltered national conversation about the Biden family's criminal pursuits.

And then the opportunity was gone.

The debate moved on to immigration and racism, and I was left thinking that the truth would never get out.

October 23–24, 2020

That Friday and Saturday, I spent most of my time waiting for the other shoe to drop. I could feel my business slipping away, and I was reluctant to venture outside my house. Thanks to the former vice president's statements in the debate, even more people were now convinced I was a Russian hacker. And even a few of my friends were now questioning my patriotism. Did they actually think I'd come to Wilmington ten years earlier and opened up a Mac repair business as a cover, just waiting for an intoxicated Hunter to one day stumble in with a damaged laptop?

History was being written to favor Joe, and my character and business were being destroyed to fit the narrative.

Then a call from Larry had me seriously fearing for my life.

October 25, 2020

Sunday was a day of reckoning. The news said that the number of early voters nine days before the election already had surpassed the total number of early voters in the 2016 election. What would happen to the country if Joe were to win? What would happen to me?

But after Larry called that evening, I had much more important things to worry about.

"Hey, JP. How are you doing? Everything OK?" he asked.

"I'm OK. Keeping my head down and my chin up."

"It's time for you to get out of town," Larry said.

My heart pounded in my chest.

"What's going on?" I asked.

"Trump is not going to win the election," Larry said. "People are taking advantage of the mail-in ballots, and it's how the election is going to be won. With Joe winning, there will be an effort to crush the *Post*'s story and everyone involved."

My breathing grew shallow.

"The new administration will cover everything up and sweep it under the carpet, and that includes you," Larry continued. "If you stay in Delaware, you will be painted as a Russian collaborator, and you will mysteriously get on a plane for Moscow after a large sum of cash is deposited in your bank account. The mainstream media will run with the story that after taking the money, you fled to Russia to be with your handlers, and that will be that. No one will ever find your body, and it will be assumed you were just another piece in Putin's plan to disrupt the 2020 election. You need to get out before the election. It's no longer safe for you to remain in Delaware."

"Understood," I replied.

Something kicked in, and instead of taking time to process this new information, I went straight into action. I called my aunt Kathy in Colorado and asked if I could stay with her for a while. She was delighted to take me in.

Kristen was heading to Florida soon to visit her parents, and maybe I could catch a ride with her to the airport. I'd call her in the morning. Then I briefed my parents on the situation, without going into details. When my father asked why I was leaving so hastily, I told him: "Larry told me it was time to get out of Dodge." It was the only thing I knew he would accept without further explanation.

"What are you going to do about the shop?" my mother asked.

I hadn't yet given it a thought; I'd been too focused on planning my departure. Her question felt like cold water splashed on my face. My ten-year effort to create a successful Mac repair business was over.

"I'm closing the shop," I said flatly. Ten years to build it, and four words to raze it to the ground.

October 26, 2020

I met up with Kristen at her house the next morning and told her what was going on.

"You're welcome to come over here before the election and camp out until Thursday," she said. "Then we can both go to the airport together."

I now had a place to go and a way to get there. All that was left was to buy a ticket and close the shop.

I had one week to move everything I wanted to keep and trash the rest. But first, with a heavy heart, I taped a notice on the inside of the glass door.

Sadly, The Mac Shop is closed for the foreseeable future. If you have a warranty issue from a previous repair, please contact the store and we will do our best to resolve the issue. We are no longer accepting new repairs. It has been an amazing 10 years being a part of this wonderful community. Thank you for everything! Cheers!

My dreams wouldn't reach their final destination. Instead it felt like they were getting kicked off at an unmarked crossing in the middle of the night. My business had weathered the worst part of COVID-19 and had even been starting to show signs of recovery, a return to normalcy. I had beaten the odds of pandemic closure only for my business to succumb to a politically motivated hit job that would take a week to bleed out.

★ 🏳 ★

Chip and my friend Tom helped me clear out the shop over the next two days. The third floor of my home, which I had lovingly remodeled for Sandy's studio, became a graveyard for my "Mac Museum" and other equipment. A wall went up between these material items and my emotions. I no longer saw potential and optimism in these boxes of parts and supplies; everything was now just old trash taking up space.

I grabbed what was worth money and discarded the rest. I thought about how easy it was to let go of what I had built over so many years, and wondered if it would have been that easy just to have discarded Hunter's laptop. If I'd done that, I wouldn't have to close my shop and leave my home.

I felt like I was being punished for having done the right thing. As if the powers that be were setting an example for others who might have the same notion.

OCTOBER 28, 2020

Instead of heading to the shop for a third day of clearing out, I was transfixed by a live broadcast of a Senate hearing. The topic: Section 230 of Title 47 of the U.S. Code, which generally provides immunity for website platforms with respect to third-party content.

Twitter's Jack Dorsey, Google's Sundar Pichai, and Facebook's Mark Zuckerberg had all been brought before the Senate to testify regarding their politically motivated actions of the previous few weeks. Zuckerberg was quick to admit there was room for improvement, saying Facebook was putting safeguards and independent fact-checkers in place, in an effort to make his platform safer and more balanced. He sounded like a guilty child trying to offer concessions to an angry parent in hopes of a more lenient punishment.

Dorsey, on the other hand, stuck to his guns. He continued to justify the company's actions in suppressing the *Post* story based on Twitter's hacked-material policy. He did acknowledge that Twitter had made a mistake in labeling the information hacked material, and said it had been a business decision. But he weaseled his way through the questioning, insisting that Twitter was not a publisher and was protected under Section 230.

But that simply wasn't true. Without knowing the truth, and only caring about the political ramifications of the *Post*'s story, Twitter had acted as a publisher and deliberately blocked the sharing of information from the American people.

I was pissed off. The balls on this guy. I picked up my phone and texted Brian, my lawyer: "I'm sitting here watching Dorsey testify before the Senate. I want you to sue the ever-loving shit out of this bearded, nose-ringed, hippie asshole."

"I was waiting for you to ask!" Brian said.

I had been suppressed, vilified, turned into a pariah. I was done being on the defensive. Brian was here to help me fight my battles. I had never intended to declare war on Twitter, but they had fired the first volley. It was now my turn to return fire.

From the high ground of Colorado, I could plan my next offensive.

October 31–November 1, 2020

That weekend at the house, I decided what I could and couldn't live without. I packed up my kilt and about a week's worth of clothes, and gathered important paperwork as well as some odds and ends. It certainly didn't feel like packing for a vacation; I felt more like a refugee fleeing with only what I could carry.

As I put my weight down on the box to get it to close, I thought that this could be all I had to start my life over with. If a riot were to break out outside my house after the election, then what was in these two bloated and overstuffed boxes, which UPS would deliver to my aunt Kathy's, might be all I'd have left.

It would have to be enough.

November 2, 2020

On the morning of my last day at the shop, I got everything together for my stay at Kristen's and the plane ride. In the afternoon, Chip and Tom helped me get the last of the trash out of the shop and clean up. Late in the evening, we loaded the last collection of boxes into Tom's pickup truck.

I turned around and faced the shop. It looked naked and exposed. The bare walls and floors reflected the light, making the room seem to glow. I hadn't removed the vinyl logo and lettering to the right of the door and on the sign above the windows. The thought of using a razor blade to scrape off the remains of my business turned my stomach. I was done. I just wanted to go home, relax, and spend the last night with my cats and friends before I had to disappear.

I figured I wouldn't ever step foot in that shop again.

★   🏴   ★

Home was quiet, and my spirits were low. The latest poll numbers showed Biden taking the lead in some swing states. I no longer feared retaliation from the Bidens. Sure, in a few years, when things had died down and all had been forgotten, I could be taken out. But for now, the Bidens would look very suspicious if something were to happen to me. I figured they were more concerned about keeping me safe from some kind of lone wolf, knowing they would take the heat for that wolf's actions.

I wasn't afraid of the FBI either. If anything, I welcomed an opportunity to have a conversation. I had a ton of questions I'd have loved to ask them.

About the only group I still feared was the CIA. Even though I'd received a lot of help by its members, I still suspected there were bad elements within the agency and felt I had to be cautious. After all, it was a spy agency, and the art of deception is a spy's greatest asset. But Larry had seemed trustworthy at every step, and anyway I had little choice but to continue to trust him.

The only people left to fear would be the lone wolves or random guys on the street. And very soon I wouldn't have to fear them either. I wouldn't be around for them to find me.

NOVEMBER 3, 2020

After a surprisingly good night's sleep, I took a shower and threw my toiletries into the large black backpack I was planning to bring to Kristen's. I topped off the cat food and gave the house a thorough once-over. There were so many improvement projects I had planned, but now they were put on hold. My home felt incomplete.

Chip and Tom were going to regularly swing by the house to check on the cats and keep an eye on the place, so I felt like my home was in good hands. If things got hairy—if riots were to break out—they were to grab the cats and nothing else.

I grabbed my bag and pulled the door shut behind me. I'd had this house for a little over six years and wasn't ready to let it go. Maybe if I maintained a foothold in Wilmington, I would be able to return once my reputation had been restored. For now, though, I had to go.

But before I could go to Kristen's, I had one last thing to do.

★ 🏳 ★

Chip and I showed up at the polls in the early afternoon; the wait was about thirty minutes. This was the most time I'd spent in public since my margarita rampage two and a half weeks earlier. I walked into the auditorium, presented my ID, signed the card, and awaited my turn to go behind the curtain and vote.

I'd never really felt like my vote mattered in Delaware, a blue state. And I already felt like this particular election had been decided months ago when the left made the push for mail-in ballots under the guise of COVID-19. But I went through the motions, as I always did, because countless brave men and women had given up their lives to afford me the right to vote. I wasn't going to disrespect what they had died for by not exercising that right.

★ 🏳 ★

At Kristen's that evening, I felt more relaxed. We grabbed some food and drinks from Añejo and settled in to watch the election results come in. But there was no outcome that night. Unbelievably, the vote tally was suspended—first in Pennsylvania, then in North Carolina, and then in Georgia.

There was still no certain outcome in the morning. Ballots were still coming in for over half the country. One thing was certain, Biden had taken the lead. As my flight grew near, I realized that I would not know who my president was until I landed. Therefore, on the plane ride, I would still not have a clear picture of what direction my life was going to take.

If President Trump were to win, I could wait until things calmed down and then slowly pick up the pieces of my former life. There would be a proper investigation, and I would be vindicated. I could return home, my community would be forced to admit they were wrong, and I would be forgiven. And ultimately, the Biden family would crumble. How long could the Bidens survive with Hunter as their patriarch? Their wealth and power would evaporate in a Las Vegas penthouse, vanishing in a cloud of crack smoke.

If Joe Biden were to win, the White House could rewrite history. And what would happen to me then? I had no idea, and I didn't really want to think about it anyway.

All I knew for certain was that I had a plane to catch.

November 5, 2020

Kristen and I headed out early so we could find a dimly lit airport bar to have a bite to eat and a few drinks. She suggested that we get an Uber to the airport using her account, so my exit from Delaware would be less documented. She had been my voice of reason for over a year, and I was so lucky to have her on my side. I will never be able to repay her for the risk she took in keeping me safe. She's the most dependable and reliable friend I have ever known. I couldn't have chosen a better friend to help me through this part of my life.

At the airport bar, the continuing tally of election votes was being broadcast on every TV screen. The election still hadn't been decided, but everyone could see where it was heading. Kristen and I quietly complained about the fairness of the election, as well as our disbelief that Joe had already surpassed Barack Obama in total votes and was on track to be the country's most popular elected president.

When we parted ways for our respective flights, our hug felt less like a fond farewell and more like uncertainty that we would ever see each other again. The walk to my terminal felt long and lonely. My life felt like a brick house that was being taken down brick by brick. Kristen was the last brick to be removed, leaving an empty border around where my life had once stood.

I settled in on the Southwest Boeing 737-700 and soon felt the gentle vibration of the turbofan lulling me to sleep. I wondered what lay ahead for me. I had hoped that by this point, the story would have had a happy ending. But it didn't have an ending at all.

I pictured in my mind the large, cinematic "To Be Continued" sign, like the one that appears at the end of the credits in *Back to the Future*.

My last thought before the wheels left the ground was, *I wonder if I'll ever get that scotch from Rudy...*

Then I drifted off.

ENDNOTES

1   Michael Kranish and David L. Stern, "As vice president, Biden said Ukraine should increase gas production. Then his son got a job with a Ukrainian gas company," *Washington Post*, July 22, 2019, https://www.washingtonpost.com/politics/as-vice-president-biden-said-ukraine-should-increase-gas-production-then-his-son-got-a-job-with-a-ukrainian-gas-company/2019/07/21/f599f42c-86dd-11e9-98c1-e945ae5db8fb_story.html.

2   Emma-Jo Morris and Gabrielle Fonrouge, "Smoking-gun email reveals how Hunter Biden introduced Ukrainian businessman to VP dad," *New York Post*, October 14, 2020, https://nypost.com/2020/10/14/email-reveals-how-hunter-biden-introduced-ukrainian-biz-man-to-dad/.

3   Elisa Shearer, "More than eight-in-ten Americans get news from digital devices," Pew Research Center, January 12, 2021, https://www.pewresearch.org/fact-tank/2021/01/12/more-than-eight-in-ten-americans-get-news-from-digital-devices/.

4   Natasha Bertrand, "Hunter Biden story is Russian disinfo, dozens of former intel officials say," *Politico*, October 19, 2020, https://www.politico.com/news/2020/10/19/hunter-biden-story-russian-disinfo-430276.

5   Presidential Debate at Belmont University in Nashville, Tennessee, October 22, 2020. The Commission on Presidential Debates, https://www.debates.org/voter-education/debate-transcripts/october-22-2020-debate-transcript/.

6   Ibid.

7   Ibid.

ACKNOWLEDGMENTS

I would like to thank everyone who supported me and stood behind me. Everyone who gave me the strength to get this far and the strength to continue to fight. Cheers!

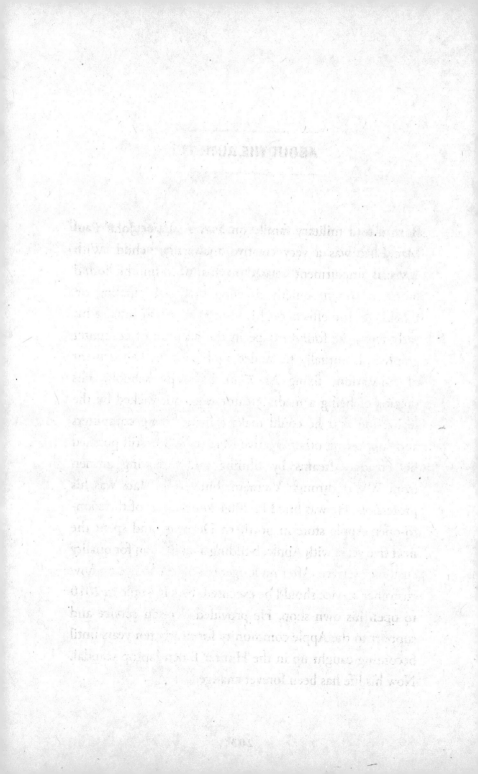

ABOUT THE AUTHOR

Born into a military family on May 3, 1976, John Paul Mac Isaac was a very creative and artistic child. With a visual impairment related to his albinism, he found more enjoyment quietly drawing than participating on a field. As the effects on his vision started to impact his early teens, he found escape in the creation of computer graphics. Eventually, he landed a job with the Department of Education, fixing Macs in Delaware schools. His dreams of being a media creator were sidetracked by the realization that he could make a living fixing computers and supporting other creative Mac users. He still pursued his creative dreams by filming and archiving airmen from WWII through Vietnam, but fixing Macs was his profession. He was hired in 2004 to be a part of the soon-to-open Apple store in northern Delaware and spent the next five years with Apple, building a reputation for quality customer service. After no longer seeing eye to eye on how customer service should be executed, he left Apple in 2010 to open his own shop. He provided five-star service and support to the Apple community for nearly ten years until becoming caught up in the Hunter Biden laptop scandal. Now his life has been forever changed.